A STRAIGHTFORWARD GUIDE
TO
BUYING AND SELLING
YOUR OWN HOME

Frances James

Straightforward Publishing
www.Straightforwardco.co.uk

Straightforward Publishing

© Straightforward Publishing 2015

British cataloguing in Publication Data. A Catalogue record of this publication is available in the British Library.

ISBN:
978-1-84716-560-2

4edge www.4edge.co.uk

Cover design by Bookworks Islington

Whilst every effort has been taken to ensure that the information contained within this book is correct at the time of going to press, the publisher and author cannot be held responsible for any errors or omissions contained within or for any subsequent changes in the law.

CONTENTS

Introduction

1. Looking for a Home   **11**

Area   11
Choosing your property   12
Valuing a property   12
Purchasing a flat   13
Leasehold Reform Act 1993   14
Viewing properties   14
Buying an old house   15
Renovation grants   16
Disabled facilities grant   16
Equalities Act 2010   16
Planning permission   16
Buying a listed building   17
Building in conservation areas   17
Buying a new home   18
Building guarantees   19
Websites   19
Buying a rented house   19
Right to buy   22
Shared Ownership   22
Self-build property   23
Key points   25

2. The Role of Estate Agents   **27**

Estate agents   27
Choosing an agent   28

Selling through more than one agent 29
Buying property using the internet 29
Selling property using the internet 30
Key points 32

3. Buying a property-The Practicalities   33

Budgeting 33
Deposits 33
Stamp duty 34
Other costs 35
Land registry 36
Energy Performance Certificates 36
Structural surveys 37
Mortgage fees 38
Buildings Insurance 38
Removals 39
Costs of moving 39
The process of buying a property 40
Making an offer 41
Putting your own home on the market 42
Exchange of contracts 42
Buying with a friend 42
Completing a purchase 43
Buying a property in an auction 43
Sale by tender 52
House swapping 53
Key points 55

4. More about mortgages   57

Lenders 57

Centralised lenders 57
Brokers and 'independent' advisors 58
How much can you borrow? 58
Mortgage market Review 59
Deposits 60
Help to Buy Scheme 61
Joint Mortgages 63
Main types of mortgages 63
What to do if given the wrong advice 66
How to complain 67
Borrowing and the internet 68
Key points 70

5. Selling your home **71**
Estate Agents 71
DIY selling 71
Setting the price 72
Selling by auction 72
Key points 79

6. Conveyancing a Property **81**
Legal ownership of property 81
Freehold property 81
Leasehold property 82
The lease 83
Check-points in a lease 85
Two systems of conveyancing 85
Registered and unregistered land 86
The key steps in conveyancing 88
Making enquiries before contract 88

Local land charges search   90
Local authority searches   91
Other searches   92
Other enquiries   93
The contract for sale   94
Procedures in the formation of a contract   95
The contents of a contract   95
Misdescription   96
Misrepresentation   96
Non-disclosure   97
Signing the contract   98
Exchanging contracts   98
Completion   98
Return of pre-contract deposits   100
The position of parties after exchange   100
Bankruptcy of the vendor   100
Bankruptcy of the purchaser   101
Death of vendor or purchaser   101
Key points   102

7. Planning Moving Arrangements   **103**
DIY moves   103
Using professionals   104
Websites   105
Contacting utilities   105

8. Buying and Selling in Scotland   **107**
Looking for property   107
Ownership of property in Scotland   107
House prices   108

The buying process   108
Surveys   108
Making an offer   109
Exchange of missives   109
Missives concluded   109
Searches   110
Selling a house or flat   110
The legal services of a solicitor   112
Accepting offers   112
Setting an entry date   113
Completion   113
Key points   115

9. Buying Overseas   **117**

General advice   117
Useful websites   118

Useful Addresses/a summary of useful websites

Index

****

INTRODUCTION

As time goes by, we either find ourselves in the middle of a housing market 'boom' or a 'bust'. Currently, at the time of writing, we are experiencing an erratic cycle in house prices, the London market is continually growing due, it is said, to a lack of new housing. Whatever the cause, home ownership is beyond the reach of many in the South East generally. Other areas are also showing signs of growth..

However, notwithstanding market conditions, the process of buying and selling a home remains probably the single most important activity undertaken by individuals in their lifetime. The money and effort involved means that it is a process that must be carried out effectively and with a clear knowledge of the elements involved.

There are different people out there buying property, some private individuals and other buy-to-let investors. This book is aimed generally at those who are trying to buy a property, whether for occupation or for investment.

When buying or selling a home, particularly buying, you will liase with a whole number of people, professional or otherwise: solicitors, estate agents, finance brokers, surveyors, banks and building societies and so on. All of these people play a vital role in the house purchase/sale transaction. All of these parties involved will have many years experience of property and not all of them will be acting in your own best interests.

Very often, the person who owns the property or who wishes to purchase a property is the one with the least knowledge of the process and is the one who stands to lose the most. When initially looking for a property, wrong decisions are made. The price paid for a property is quite often too high, with disastrous consequences later on. The condition of the property may leave a lot to be desired. There are many stories of people losing out on this single most important transaction. Unfortunately, it is a fact that if mistakes are made at the outset then you might spend the rest of your life recovering from the consequences.

This book also covers buying a property abroad and is meant to be of help to those who have decided to invest in a property overseas for one reason or another. Like all areas of life, knowledge is a precious asset and can help you make informed decisions. This book will go some way to assist you in being able to make informed decisions and to understand more about the process of buying and selling a property.

****

1

Buying a Home-Looking for a Home

Obviously, where you choose to buy your house will be your own decision. However, it may be your first time and you may be at a loss as to where to buy, i.e. rural areas or urban areas, the type and cost of property or whether a house or flat. There are several considerations here:

Area

Buying in a built up area has its advantages and disadvantages. There are normally more close communities, because of the sheer density. However, it is true to say that some built up areas have become fragmented by population movement, "Yuppification" etc. Local services are closer to hand and there is a greater variety of housing for sale. Transport links are also usually quite good and there are normally plenty of shops.

Disadvantages are less space, less privacy, more local activity, noise and pollution, less street parking, more expensive insurance and different schooling to rural environments. The incidence of crime and vandalism and levels of overall stress are higher in built up, more urban areas. This is not the case with all built up areas. It is up to the buyer to carry out research before making a commitment. If you are considering buying in a rural area, you might want to consider the following: there is more detached housing with land, more space and privacy. However, this can be undermined by the "village" syndrome where everyone knows your business, or wants to know your business. There is also cleaner air and insurance premiums can be lower. Disadvantages can be isolation, loneliness, lower level of services generally, and a limited choice of local education.

Choosing your property

You should think carefully when considering purchasing a larger property. You may encounter higher costs, which may include:

- Larger, more expensive, carpeting
- More furniture. It is highly unlikely that your existing furniture will suit a new larger home.
- Larger gardens to tend. Although this may have been one of the attractions, large gardens are time consuming, expensive and hard work.
- Bigger bills
- More decorating
- Higher overall maintenance costs

Valuing a property

In the main, buyers will leave it to estate agents to offer a fair price, or market price for the house. In a period of spiralling house price inflation which is now thankfully over, although there was a re-occurrence of this in London, values were seemingly plucked out of the air. If you want to compare estate agents valuations with others then you can access one of the websites, such as www.hometrack or rightmove in order to gain a comparative value. Other sites are the

Halifax, Nationwide, the Royal Institute of Chartered Surveyors, the National Association of Estate Agents and the Land Registry. You can also gain an idea of the valuation by looking in estate agents windows and assessing similar properties.

Purchasing a flat

There are some important points to remember when purchasing a flat. These are common points that are overlooked. If you purchase a flat in a block, the costs of maintenance of the flat will be your own. However, the costs of maintaining the common parts will be down to the landlord (usually) paid for by you through a service charge. There has been an awful lot of trouble with service charges, trouble between landlord and leaseholder. It has to be said that many landlords see service charges as a way of making profit over and above other income, such as ground rent, which is usually negligible after sale of a lease.

Many landlords will own the companies that carry out the work and retain the profit made by these companies. They will charge leaseholders excessively for works which are often not needed. The 1996 Housing Act (as amended by the Commonhold and Leasehold Reform Act 2002) attempts to strengthen the hand of leaseholders against unscrupulous landlords by making it very difficult indeed for landlords to take legal action for forfeiture (repossession) of a lease without first giving the leaseholder a chance to challenge the service charges.

Be very careful if you are considering buying a flat in a block – you should establish levels of service charges and look at accounts. Try to elicit information from other leaseholders. It could be that there is a leaseholders organisation, formed to manage their own service charges. This will give you direct control over contracts such as gardening, cleaning, maintenance contacts and cyclical decoration contracts. Better value for money is obtained in this way. In this case, at least you know that the levels will be fair, as no one leaseholder stands to profit.

Leasehold Reform Act 1993 as amended by the Commonhold and Leasehold Reform Act 2002

Under this Act, all leaseholders have the right to extend the length of their lease by a term of 90 years. For example, if your lease has 80 years left to run you can extend it to 170 Years. There is a procedure in the above Act for valuation. Leaseholders can also collectively purchase the freehold of the block. There is a procedure for doing this in the Act although it is often time consuming and can be expensive. There are advantages however, particularly when leaseholders are not satisfied with management.

Viewing properties

Before you start house hunting, draw up a list of characteristics you will need from your new home, such as the number of bedrooms, size of kitchen, garage, study and garden. Take the estate agents details with you when viewing. Also, take a tape measure with you. Assess the location of the property. Look at all the aspects and the surroundings. Give some thought as to the impact this will have in your future life. Assess the building, check the facing aspect of the property, i.e., north, south etc. and check the exterior carefully. Earlier, I talked about the need to be very careful when assessing a property. When you have made your mind up, a survey is essential.

Look for a damp proof course - normally about 15cm from the ground. Look for damp inside and out. Items like leaking rainwater pipes should be noted, as they can be a cause of damp. Look carefully at the windows. Are they rotten? Do they need replacing and so on. Look for any cracks. These should most certainly be investigated. A crack can be symptomatic of something worse or it can merely be surface. If you are not in a position to make this judgement then others should make it for you.

Heating is important. If the house or flat has central heating you will need to know when it was last tested. Gas central heating should be tested at least once a year.

All in all you need to remember that you cannot see everything in a house, particularly on the first visit. A great deal may be being concealed from you. In addition, your own knowledge of property may be slim. A second opinion is a must.

Buying an old house

If you are considering purchasing an older house and making improvements then there are a number of things to think about: consider whether your proposed alterations will be in keeping with the age and style of the house, and neighbouring houses, particularly in a terrace. A classic mistake is that of replacing doors and windows with unsympathetic modern products. Again, salesmen will sell you anything and quite often won't provide the correct advice. If appropriate, you should consider contacting the Victorian Society or the Georgian Group for advice on preserving your home. Both offer leaflets to help you carry out appropriate restoration. It is often a good idea to employ an architect or surveyor to oversee any alterations you are considering. For local contractors contact the Royal Institute of British Architects or Royal Institute of Chartered Surveyors.

Renovation grants

These may be available from local authorities, although there are stringent requirements. They are means tested and the higher your income the more you are expected to pay. For further details you should contact your local authority direct.

Disabled facilities grant

A grant may be available to adapt a property for a disabled person, for example improving access into and around the home and adapting existing facilities within it. These grants are mandatory, but a discretionary grant is available to make a property suitable for the accommodation, welfare or employment of a disabled person. A leaflet, generally entitled Help for Disabled People with Adaptation and Other works, which can be obtained from your local authority, provides basic information.

Equalities Act 2010

The Equality Act 2010, with effect from October 2010, has introduced an obligation on all landlords to ensure that, if a disabled person requests it, suitable disabled access to common parts, and within common parts is available. Again, information is available from the local authority.

Planning permission

If you are considering alterations of a significant nature, either internal or external, you may need planning permission from your local authority. You may need planning permission if you plan to change the look or external aspect of the building or if you are intending to change the use.

You are allowed to carry out some work without planning permission, so it is worth contacting the local authority. You should also ask about building regulations. These are concerned with the materials and methods of building adopted. Regulations for work carried out in conservation areas are strict. The building control department at your local authority will be able to advise you about building regulations.

Buying a listed building

Buildings of architectural or historical interest are listed by the Secretary of State for National Heritage following consultation with English Heritage, to protect them against inappropriate alteration. In Wales, buildings are listed by the Secretary of State for Wales in consultation with CADW (Heritage Wales). In Scotland, they are listed by the Secretary of State for Scotland, in consultation with Historic Scotland. If you intend to carry out work to a listed building, you are likely to need listed building consent for any internal or external work, in addition to planning permission. The conservation officer in the local planning department can provide further information.

Buildings in conservation areas

Local authorities can designate areas of special architectural or historical significance. Conservation areas are protected to ensure that their character or interest is retained. Whole towns or villages may be conservation areas or simply one particular street. Strict regulations are

17

laid down for conservation areas. Protection includes all buildings and all types of trees that are larger than 7cm across at 1.5m above the ground. There may be limitations for putting up signs, outbuilding or items such as satellite dishes. Any developments in the area usually have to meet strict criteria, such as the use of traditional or local materials.

This also applies to property in national parks, designated Areas of Outstanding Natural Beauty and the Norfolk or Suffolk Broads.

Whether or not a property is listed or is deemed to be in a conservation area will show up when your conveyancer carries out the local authority search.

Buying a new house

There are a number of benefits to buying a new house. You have the advantages of being the first occupants. There should not be a demand for too much maintenance or DIY jobs, as the building is new. There will, however, be a defects period which usually runs for 6 months for building and 12 months for electrical mechanical. During this period you should expect minor problems, such as cracking of walls, plumbing etc, which will be the responsibility of the builder.

Energy loss will be minimal. A new house today uses 50 per cent less energy than a house built 15 years ago; consider the savings over an older property. An energy rating indicates how energy efficient a house is. The National House Building Council uses a rating scheme based on the National Energy Services Scheme, in which houses are giving a rating between 0 and 10. A house rated 10 will be very energy efficient and have very low running costs for its size. Security and safety are built in to new houses, smoke alarms are standard and security locks on doors and windows are usually included.

When the house market is slow developers usually offer incentives to buyers, such as cashback, payment of deposit etc. Sometimes they offer a part exchange scheme. These are definitely worth looking into. However, with part exchange you may not get the price you were looking for.

Building Guarantees

All new houses should be built to certain standards and qualify for one of the building industry guarantees. These building guarantees are normally essential for you to obtain a mortgage and they also make the property attractive to purchasers when you move. A typical Guarantee is the National Housebuilding Council Guarantee (NHBC).

Websites for housebuilders

Most developers have their own websites with details and picture of their developments. These include both new properties and refurbished. In addition there are several websites that specialise in new properties only. One such site is www.newhomesnetwork.co.uk

Buying a Rented House-Right to Buy

If you rent your house from your council, you will be able to buy it at a discount under Right to Buy legislation. the current government has increased discounts in an attempt to increase the right to buy. If you live in a new town, a housing association or housing association trust, you would need to make enquiries, as many are exempt, although the government announced that it was introducing legislation to force Housing Associations to sell properties under the right to buy. A compromise has been reached where this will be voluntary. The following rules apply to the Right to Buy:

- You get a 35% discount if you've been a public sector tenant for between 3 and 5 years.
- After 5 years, the discount goes up by 1% for every extra year you've been a public sector tenant, up to a maximum of 70% – or £77,900 across England and £103,900 in London boroughs (whichever is lower).

Flats

- You get a 50% discount if you've been a public sector tenant for between 3 and 5 years.
- After 5 years, the discount goes up by 2% for every extra year you've been a public sector tenant, up to a maximum of 70% – or £77,900 across England and £103,900 in London boroughs (whichever is lower).

If your landlord has spent money on your home

Your discount will be less if your landlord has spent money building or maintaining your home:

- in the last 10 years - if your landlord built or acquired your home before 2 April 2012
- in the last 15 years - if you're buying your home through Preserved Right to Buy, or if your landlord acquired your home after 2 April 2012

You won't get any discount if your landlord has spent more money than your home is now worth.

Social Homebuy

With Social HomeBuy, you buy a share of your council or housing association home and pay rent on the rest of it.

To apply, ask your landlord for an application form.

Discounts

You'll get a discount of between £9,000 and £16,000 on the value of your home, depending on:

- where your home is

- the size of the share you're buying

If you want to buy another share in your home later on, you'll get a discount on that too.

Buying more of your home later

You must buy at least 25% of your home. You can buy more later, until you own 100%. This is called 'staircasing'.

If you buy more of your home, your rent will go down - because it's based on how much of the property you rent. Your landlord can charge rent of up to 3% of the value of their share of your home, per year.

ExampleYour home is worth £240,000 and you buy a 50% share. Your landlord charges you 3% rent on their 50% share. 3% of £120,000 is £3,600 per year. This works out at £300 per month for you to pay in rent.

Who can't apply

You can't use Social HomeBuy if:

- you have an <u>assured shorthold tenancy</u>

- you're being made <u>bankrupt</u>

- a court has <u>ordered you to leave your home</u>

- your landlord is taking action against you for rent arrears, anti-social behaviour or for breaking your tenancy agreement

Not all local councils or housing associations have joined the scheme. Check with your landlord to find out if they belong to the scheme and whether your home is included

Help to Buy Scheme

See chapter 4 for more details on Help to Buy and how it might benefit you.

Shared/part ownership property

There are properties available on a shared/part ownership basis, usually from housing associations. Local Authorities also provide such schemes, although rarely. The main principle is that you buy a percentage of the property, say 50% and you rent the rest, with a service charge if a flat. As time goes by you can "staircase up" to 100% ownership. This is a scheme specially designed for those who cannot meet the full cost of outright purchase in the first instance. Usually, your total monthly outgoings are smaller than they would be if you purchased outright. Social Housing providers run a range of different schemes each year, largely depending on Government requirements. For further details you should contact a large housing association in your area who will provide you with current schemes on offer and point you in the right direction.

Self-build property

Self-build is another option for obtaining a new home. However, it is time consuming and not for the faint hearted. You need to be organised and to have organised the finances and your work programme. Usually the biggest problem is finding a suitable plot of land. There is a lot of competition. It also means that you will, unless you employ an agent, be charged with supervising a number of skilled craftsmen. Self-build usually works out cheaper than buying off a developer but it is certainly not an easy option. For more information and advice check out the following websites:

www.homebuilding.co.uk
This is run by the publishers of homebuilding and renovation magazine which is the leading magazine for homebuilders. The site is magazine style with lots of articles and also a link to www.plotfinder.net. This is a recently established database of land for sale and houses to renovate. There is an annual subscription cost, currently £39.15 (as at 2014/2015)

www.buildstore.co.uk
This site is owned by a group of venture capitalists, individuals and companies involved in the self build market. Again, there is a mix of articles and also adverts.

www.ebuild.co.uk
This site is published by specialist publisher's webguides on line. The

site includes a directory of suppliers from architectural salvage to waste disposal with links to useful sites.

www.npbs.co.uk
This is the site of Norwich and Peterborough Building Society, who offer mortgages for self build projects. The loan for self-build is released in stages linked to the building of the property. It is worth checking to see if these mortgages are on offer.

Now read the Key Points from Chapter 1 Overleaf.

****

Key Points From Chapter One

- When looking for a house, consider essential points such as area and services.

- Think carefully about costs involved and also work if you are considering buying a larger property.

- When purchasing a flat, consider maintenance charges.

- Before viewing, draw up a list of characteristics you will need from a house or flat.

- There are a number of advantages to buying a new house, such as new construction and minimal energy loss.

- Other schemes available include self-build housing

2

The Role of Estate Agents in Buying and Selling Property

Estate Agents

Estate agents are the normal route to buying or selling a home, although, as we will see later, online agents are prospering, offering cheaper deals for the sale or purchase of a property, many doing it for a fixed fee. However, a lot of people like the 'personal touch' and use agents.

There are things to watch out for, particularly in London, where there is a big demand and short supply. Estate agents will often try to charge various 'fees' for services and tie people into different charges in the contract. Always demand to know the fees and be sure where you are before you enter into a contract.

What to expect from an estate agent:

- Advice on the selling or asking price of a house or flat - they know the local market
- Advice on the best way to sell (or buy) and where to advertise; they should discuss an advertising budget with you
- If selling, a meeting to visit, assess and value your home and also to take down the particulars of your home. The Property Misdescriptions Act 2010, which arose out of the bad old days of the 1980's, prevents agents from using ambiguous statements to

enhance the sale of the property. You should look at the points carefully as people who are disappointed after reading such a glowing report will not purchase.

- They may ask for details of recent bills, such as council tax and electricity. They should also be willing to give advice on fixtures and fittings included in the sale.
- They should be willing to show potential buyers around your home if you are not available.
- Don't expect to have to pay for a for-sale board although some lenders will try to make a charge.

Although a seller does not have any specific duty to disclose information about a property, estate agents have specific legal obligations not to mislead members of the public. Since 2013 agents have been covered by the general duties owed by other businesses to consumers that are set out in the Consumer Protection from Unfair Trading Regulations 2008. These regulations include a ban on misleading statements or omissions and they effectively require estate agents to reveal any material facts about a property to potential buyers.

Choosing an agent if selling

Consider the following points:

- They ought to sell your type of property or specialise in one particular area of the market
- They should be a member of one of the professional bodies such as the National Association of Estate Agents, the Royal Institution of Chartered Surveyors, The Incorporated Society of Valuers and Auctioneers, The Architects and Surveyors Institute or the Association of Building Engineers.. Get quotes of fees, including:

- the basic charge and any extras you might have to pay for, such as advertising in specialist publications.

Choose at least two agents to value the house, if instructing an agent.

Sole agency selling.

Offering an agent sole agency may reduce the fee. This can be done for a limited time. After this you can instruct multiple agents. With sole agency you can sell privately, although you may still be liable for the sole agent's fee.

Joint sole agents

With this arrangement, two or more agents co-operate in the house sale and split the commission. The agents may charge a higher commission in this case.

Multiple agency

This means that you have several agents trying to sell your home, but only pay the agent who sells your property.

Buying property using the internet

There are a number of websites that also detail properties, some are independent and some are owned by the large players.

The following are a selection of the main sites:
www.rightmove.co.uk.

This is one of the largest sites, jointly owned and run by Halifax, Royal Sun Alliance, Connell and Countryside assured Group. They jointly claim to represent more than 170,000 properties covering 99% of UK postcodes. The main function of this site is as a property search site, enabling people to search for property by name of area and postcode.

Each property has a reference number and will have a photo and details. These can be obtained by clicking on the property. There is much useful information, including room sizes.

www.zoopla.co.uk
The claims of this website are that it can help the buyer to find a property, move home and settle in.

www.primelocation.co.uk
This site was launched in 2000 by a consortium of estate agents. This site deals with more expensive properties.

Selling property using the internet

Although estate agents are still the main avenues for selling property, as we have seen, the web now plays a more significant part. In addition to the websites detailed, almost all agents now have their own website. This is really an electronic shop window where your property is displayed. Buyers interested in your property should be able to e-mail the estate agent directly for a viewing.

Ten top tips when selling a property

If you are selling a property, there are a number of things that you need to get right in order to ensure the best chance on the market:

- Get the price right-this is absolutely crucial-if you try to overprice then you will harm your chances of a sale as you will lose the trust of would-be purchasers-pitch the price attractively.
- Make your property presentable-remember that you are selling your home and you should show it to its best advantage.
- get the photos right
- make sure it is described fully-do not mss anything out.
- make your agent work for you. the first 30 days on the property market are crucial. make sure you are in regular contact with
- them.
- Don't forget to include a floor plan.
- make sure you have all the relevant certificates and paperwork, such as gas and electricity certificates, and damp proofing etc.

This advice applies whether you are using a traditional high street agent or are using an online agent. make sure that what you are selling is shown in its best light.

Now read the key points from chapter 2.

****

Key points from chapter 2

- Estate agents have a number of roles. However, the main function is to guide the buyer/seller through the process from beginning to end.

- Make sure that you choose the appropriate agent if selling. Make sure that the agent is a member of a professional body.

- You will need to consider whether you wish to sell through more than one estate agent.

- There are a number of websites dealing with buying and selling property. This is often a cheaper way of purchasing or selling.

- Make sure that you show all the features of your property in the best light.

3

Buying a Property-The Practicalities

Considerations when buying a house or flat

Budgeting

Before beginning to look for a house you need to sit down and give careful thought to the costs involved in the whole process. The starting point is to identify the different elements in the overall transaction.

Deposits

Sometimes the estate agent will ask you for a small deposit when you make the offer (see Estate Agents, chapter 2). This indicates that you are serious about the offer and is a widespread and legitimate practice, as long as the deposit is not too much, £100 is usual. The main deposit for the property, i.e., the difference between the mortgage and what has been accepted for the property, isn't paid until the exchange of contracts. Once you have exchanged contracts on a property the purchase is legally binding. Until then, you are free to withdraw. The deposit cannot be reclaimed after exchange.

Until recently, and the onset of the recession, banks would normally lend up to 95% of the purchase price of the property. However, particularly now, even though a few banks are willing to lend up to 95% the less you borrow the more favourable terms you can normally get from bank or building society. It has to be said that in the period leading up to the 'credit crunch' we were in a situation where banks loaned money to all and sundry at up to 125% of the value of the home plus exaggerated income multiples. Banks have now tightened up their lending criteria considerably. Recently, The Mortgage Market review came into effect (2014) which has imposed further restrictions on banks and building society lending and requires a stringent set of checks carried out before a mortgage is approved. All lenders insist on larger minimum deposits. This will vary with the bank or building society and you should also scan the Sunday newspapers in particular for details of best buys for mortgages. Refer to the previous chapter for details on help to buy, with the government guaranteeing deposits.

Stamp duty- What is stamp duty and who pays it?

Stamp Duty — Stamp Duty Land Tax (SDLT) official jargon — is a tax you pay when you buy a home. The buyer pays stamp duty – not the person selling. Stamp duty applies to both freehold and leasehold purchases over £125,000

2. How much do I have to pay?

Stamp duty used to be charged on the whole property price, so that it went up in big jumps. For example, if you bought a property for £250,000 you would have paid £2500 stamp duty; but if you bought a house costing just £1 more, you would tip into the next stamp duty bracket (what used to be 3%) and pay £7500 – a £5000 jump. This slab structure is gone now and from December 4, 2014 stamp duty is applied like income tax.

Stamp duty is charged according to the scale overleaf.

Purchase price of property	Stamp duty rate
Up to £125,000	Zero
Over £125,000 to £250,000	2%
Over £250,000 to £925,000	5%
Over £925,000 to £1.5 million	10%
Over £1.5 million	12%

So, for example, if the agreed purchase price is £275,000, under the new rules, stamp duty is calculated.
0% on the first £125,000 = £0
2% on the next £125,000 = £2,500
5% on the final £ 25,000 = £1,250
Total stamp duty payable = £3,750

Tax for properties held offshore

HMRC has announced in March 2013, that an annual levy will now be made on properties held in British and Offshore companies, costing £2million or more. This is a measure to tackle tax avoidance. Those homes valued at between £2m-£5m will have to pay £15,000 per year; those between £5m-£10m will be taxed at £35,000; those with values of between £10m-£20m will pay £70,000 per year. owners of homes above £20m per year will have to pay £140,000 per year.

Whilst this is not likely to affect readers of this book, it is always better to be aware of such changes.

Other costs

A solicitor normally carries out conveyancing of property. However, it is perfectly normal for individuals to do their own conveyancing. All the necessary paperwork can be obtained from legal stationers and it is executed on a step-by-step basis. It has to be said that solicitors are now very competitive with their charges and, for the sake of between £600-£900, it is better to let someone else do the work which allows you to concentrate on other things.

Land Registry

The Land Registry records all purchases of land in England and Wales and is open to the public (inspection of records, called a property search). The registered title to any particular piece of land or property will carry with it a description and include the name of owner, mortgage, rights over other persons land and any other rights. There is a small charge for inspection. A lot of solicitors have direct links and can carry out searches very quickly. Not all properties are registered although it is now a duty to register all transactions. (See chapter 6, conveyancing)

Energy Performance Certificates (EPC's)

EPC's are compulsory. An EPC surveyor will assess the property and looks at all the ways a house or flat can waste heat, such as inadequate loft insulation, lack of cavity wall insulation, draughts and obsolete boilers. After the assessment they will award a rating from A (as good as it gets) to G (terrible). The document also includes information and advice on how to improve matters, such as lagging the water tank or installing double-glazing. An EPC will cost between £120-130 and will be valid for ten years. Improvements made while the certificate is in force will not need a new survey. However, watch out for companies that offer them for higher prices. Always search around.

Structural surveys

The basic structural survey is the homebuyers survey and valuation which is normally carried out by the building society or other lender. This will cost you between £250-£500 and is not really an in-depth survey, merely allowing the lender to see whether they should lend or not, and how much they should lend. Sometimes, lenders keep what they refer to as a retention, which means that they will not forward the full value (less deposit) until certain defined works have been carried out. If you want to go further than a homebuyers report then you will have to instruct a firm of surveyors who have several survey types, depending on how far you want to go and how much you want to spend.

A word of caution. Many people go rushing headlong into buying a flat or house. They are usually exhilarated and wish to complete their purchase fairly quickly in order to establish their new home. If you stop and think about this, it is complete folly and can prove very expensive later. A house or flat is a commodity, like other commodities, except that it is usually a lot more expensive. A lot can be wrong with the commodity that you have purchased which is not immediately obvious. Only after you have completed the deal and paid over the odds for your purchase do you begin to regret what you have done.

The true price of a property is not what the estate agent is asking, certainly not what the seller is asking. The true market price is the difference between what a property in good condition is being sold at and your property minus cost of works to bring it up to that value. Therefore, if you have any doubts whatsoever, and if you can afford it get a detailed survey of the property you are proposing to buy and get the works required costed out. When negotiating, this survey is an essential tool in order to arrive at an accurate and fair price. Do not rest faith in others, particularly when you alone stand to lose.

One further word of caution. As stated, a lot of problems with property cannot be seen. A structural survey will highlight those. In some cases it may not be wise to proceed at all.

Mortgage fees

Mortgage indemnity insurance. This is a one-off payment if you are arranging a mortgage over 70-80% of lenders valuation. This represents insurance taken out by the lender in case the purchaser defaults on payments, in which case the lender will sell the property to reclaim the loan. It is to protect the mortgage lender not the buyer. The cost of the insurance varies depending on how much you borrow. A 90% mortgage on a £60,000 property will cost between £300-600. For a 100% mortgage it is usually much higher. You have to ask yourself, if you are paying up to £2,000 for this kind of insurance on a 100% mortgage, is it not better to try to raise the money to put down a bigger deposit. Always think about the relative economics. A lot of money is made by a lot of people in house buying and selling. The loser is usually the buyer or seller, not the host of middlemen. So think carefully about what you are doing.

Mortgage arrangement fees

Depending upon the type of mortgage you are considering you may have to pay an arrangement fee. You should budget for a minimum of £400.

Buildings insurance

When you have purchased your property you will need to take out buildings insurance. This covers the cost of rebuilding your home if it is damaged. It also covers the cost of subsidence, storm and flood damage, burst pipes and other water leaks and vandalism and third party damage generally. The insurance company will tell you more about elements covered. It is worth shopping around for buildings insurance as prices vary significantly.

Many banks/building societies also supply buildings insurance if you arrange a mortgage with them. You shouldn't immediately take up their offer, as they are not always the most competitive. Websites such as www.confused.com can provide a range of quotes for you.

Removals

Unless you are not moving far and are considering doing it yourself, you should budget for hiring a removal firm. This will depend on how many possessions you have and how much time and money you have. Take care when choosing the removal firm. Choose one who comes recommended if possible. There are other costs too. Reconnection of telephone lines and possibly a deposit, carpets, curtains and plumbing-in washing machines. How much you pay will probably depend on how handy you are yourself. There are also smaller incidental costs such as redirecting mail by the post office. We will be discussing moving home in more depth later on in chapter 8.

Costs of moving

The table below will give you an idea of typical costs, such as solicitors fees, stamp duty, land registry fees and search fees when buying a property. The costs are based on a purchase of a typical London property. Other costs as discussed above will be extra. It has to be stressed that, apart from the stamp duty and Land Registry Fees (which should be checked) solicitor's costs and searches will vary. Searches will cost more in different areas and solicitors fees will come down.

House price	Solicitors fees (av)	Stamp duty	Land Registry	Search fees	Total fees
£150,000	£900	£500	200	200	1800
£200,000	£900	£1500	200	200	£2800
£300,000	£1000	5000	280	235	6,515
£500,000	£1000	15,000	280	280	16,560
£750,000	1069	27,500	280	280	29129
£1m	1372	66250	920	235	68777
£1.5m	1895	116,500	920	235	119550
£2m	2208	166,500	920	235	169863
£2.5m	2723	236500	920	235	240378
£3m	3656	260,000	920	235	264811
£3.5m	4231	310,000	920	235	315386
£4m	4871	360,000	920	235	366026

The process of buying a property

Having considered the basic elements of buying a property, the next step is to find the property you want. As we have discussed, this is a long and sometimes dispiriting process. Trudging around estate agents, sorting through mountains of literature, dealing with mountains of estate agents details, scouring the papers and walking the streets! However, most of us find the property we want at the end of the day. It is then that we can put in our offer. One useful way of determining the respective values of property in different areas is to visit a website set up for that purpose www.hometrack.co.uk. This particular site collects price information from selected estate agents in different postcode areas across the country. At the time of writing, prices are currently available for London and the southeast, the southwest, Birmingham and the Midlands and the north of England. Before you decide to look, a little research into prices and comparisons with what you can afford might be useful.

Making an offer

You should put your offer in to the estate agent or direct to the seller, depending who you are buying from. As discussed earlier, your offer should be based on sound judgement, on what the property is worth not on your desire to secure the property at any cost. A survey will help you to arrive at a schedule of works and cost. If you cannot afford to employ a surveyor from a high street firm then you should try to enlist other help. In addition, you should take a long and careful look at the house yourself, not just a cursory glance. Look at everything and try to get an idea of the likely cost to you of rectifying defects. However, I cannot stress enough the importance of getting a detailed survey. Eventually, you will be in a position to make an offer for the property.

You should base this offer on sound judgement and you should provide a rationalisation for your offer, if it is considerably lower than the asking price. You should make it clear that your offer is subject to contract and survey (if you require further examination or wish to carry out a survey after the offer).

Putting your own home on the market

Most people moving try to secure the sale of their own home before looking for a new one. If you haven't started to sell your house yet, you are advised to do so as soon as possible. You need also to arrange finance. A lot of people have had the nightmarish experience of stepping into an estate agents and being besieged by "independent" financial advisors wishing to sell you their product. Be very careful at this stage. See "getting your mortgage" chapter 5.

Exchange of contracts

Once the buyer and seller are happy with all the details stated in the contract and your conveyancer can confirm that there are no outstanding legal queries, those conveyancing will exchange contracts. The sale is now legally binding for both parties. You should arrange the necessary insurances, buildings and contents from this moment on as you are now responsible for the property.

Buying with a friend

The 1996 Family Law Act brought in the concept of cohabiting couples having the same rights as married couples. This will apply particularly if your marriage starts to break up and you wish to ascertain property rights. However, it is wise to draw up a cohabitation contract prior to purchase which will put in writing how the property is shared and will make clear the situation after break-up. The cohabitation contract can include any conditions you wish and is drawn up usually by a solicitor. There are standard forms for cohabitation agreements which can include financial arrangements stating who pays for the mortgage, who can call for a sale, mutual wills, and who pays for and owns possessions. You can obtain a leaflet concerning this from a Citizens Advice Bureau or from a solicitor.

Completing a sale

This is the final day of the sale and normally takes place around ten days after Exchange. Exchange and completion can take place on the same day if necessary but this is unusual. On day of completion, you are entitled to vacant possession and will receive the keys. See chapter 6 for more details on the conveyancing process.

Buying at auction

Although many people will go through the traditional route of acquiring property through an estate agent, there are other routes, one main one being the auction. Buying at auction requires a different set of skills and you need to know what you are buying, where it is and what the problems are, if any.

Why is it being sold at auction? Certainly, you need to act fairly quickly as you need to inspect the property before auction day, arrive at the final bid price that you will not exceed and be prepared to complete within 28 days.

What is a property auction?

The process is very similar to the normal method of private sale. However, for an auction sale the seller and their solicitor carry out all the necessary paperwork and legal investigations prior to the auction. Subject to the property receiving an acceptable bid, the property will be 'sold' on auction day with a legally binding exchange of contracts and a fixed completion date.

Different types of property auction houses

Auction houses vary in size and the amount of business that they conduct and the frequency with which they hold auctions. Most will sell both residential and commercial property and each will have its own style of operation, and fee structure. Large auction houses will hold auctions frequently, perhaps every two months and will have around 250 lots for sale. A lot of the auctions happen in London. Most of the large auction houses will deal with property put forward by large institutions, such as banks selling repossessions.

Also local authorities and will advertise the sales in the mainstream media and trade papers. The medium size auction houses will hold auctions as frequently as they can, in regional venues, such as racecourses and conference centres, and depending on stock, usually every two to three months, tending to advertise locally. The small auction houses will have far fewer lots and will hold their sales in smaller local venues. They may advertise in local press but more often will trade on word of mouth.

Those who attend auctions

As you might imagine, all sorts of people attend auctions. The common denominator is that they are all interested in buying property.

Property investors are most common at auction, people who are starting out building a portfolio or those who have large portfolios that they wish to expand. They tend to fall into two groups, those who are after capital appreciation, i.e. buy at a low value and build the capital value and those who are looking for rental income. Then there are the property traders who like a quick profit from buying and 'flipping' property. These types usually have intimate knowledge of an area and are well placed to make a quick profit. Then we have the developers who look for small profitable sites or larger sites where property can be built and sold on. The sites can have existing buildings on them or can be vacant lots with or without planning permission. Last, but not least, we have those people who intend to buy solely for the purpose of owner occupation, look to buy a below- value property that they can redesign and make their own.

What types of property are suitable for auction?

There is strong demand for all types of properties offered at auction. These may be properties requiring updating, those with short leases, development sites with or without planning permission, repossessions, forced sales and, investment properties. Also ground rents, probates, receivership sales and local authority properties.

However, any type of property can be sold at auction and initially the property will be inspected to discuss specific criteria and the current situation. Extensive research will be carried out by the auction house and advice offered as to whether auction is the appropriate method of sale. The below represents a cross section of what might be found at auction.

Properties for Improvement

Properties in need of updating make ideal auction Lots. They are in great demand from refurbishment specialists and private buyers, keen to undertake a project for their own occupation or for resale. They also appeal to buy-to-let investors who carry out the improvements then retain them as part of a property portfolio.

Tenanted Properties

Residential houses and flats with tenants in residence sell well at auction. Notice doesn't need to be served on tenants, and rental income continues to be received right up to completion.

Residential Investments

Houses in multiple occupation and blocks of flats are sold at auction as valuable investments. Here it is the rent level that determines the sale price, just as much as the building itself.

Development Propositions

Derelict or disused farm buildings, empty commercial premises, buildings with potential for conversion or change of use, can all sell well at auction. In some locations a change to residential can significantly add to the value of a property, in other situations there may be space for additional dwellings or to substantially enlarge the property.

Building Land

There is no better way of ensuring a seller achieves best price for a building plot or parcel of development land than to offer it for sale by auction. Builders will be able to consult with architects, planners etc., and be ready to bid in the auction room.

Mixed-Use Properties

Properties that have twin uses or a variety of potential future uses are ideal for sale by auction. Retail shops with accommodation above appeal to investors as well as owner-occupiers. Further conversion work can often be undertaken and the property tailored to suit the purchaser's special requirements.

Commercial Investments

Retail shops, offices, industrial units, garage blocks and parking areas - an ever increasing number of commercial investments are being sold at auction. It doesn't matter whether they are vacant or tenanted, with lease renewal soon needed or with a long way to run.

Unique Properties

There are always some rare entries, sought after property and prime locations that need to be sold in a competitive bidding environment. Unexpectedly high prices have been achieved by this route.

Amenity Land and Other Property

Paddocks, meadows, fields, moorings, amenity land and also other unusual land parcels are all sold at auction. If it is property or land that is surplus to requirements, the likelihood is a buyer can be found at auction.

Why is property being sold at an auction?
There are a number of reasons why property is sold at an auction:

- A quick sale is needed, often due to the owner being in financial difficulties or it is a repossession
- There are structural problems which prevent the property being sold easily in the conventional manner.
- Properties sold by public bodies. Here you get all sort of property, including weird and wonderful properties such as public toilets and police stations, all of which may have their uses.
- The property is unique and there are no direct comparisons, such as lighthouses and the above mentioned public toilet.

It is always best to find out why exactly the property is being sold at auction. Is it so difficult to get rid of because of some inherent reason? Ask why is this property at auction and not being sold in the conventional way? Who exactly is the vendor and what if any are the problems stopping it being sold conventionally? The reasons that the property is at auction may be entirely innocent but it is always worth finding out to avoid future problems.

What happens next?

Once you have found your auction, to receive a complimentary auction catalogue you should contact the Auctioneers and this will give the information about the properties being offered for sale. You can also download a catalogue from the auctioneers website. The catalogue includes descriptions of the available properties, legal information, viewing arrangements and a guide price, which is purely an indication of a realistic selling price. This should not be taken as a firm asking or selling price and should be relied upon as a guide only. Professional advice must be taken in relation to any lot in which there is an interest.

For lots where viewings are arranged, these are carried out on a block basis and are published in all advertising and in the auction catalogue.

Any prospective purchaser is welcome at these viewings and should the scheduled appointments be inconvenient, alternative arrangements can be made. Any interest must be registered with the Auctioneers in order that prospective purchasers may be kept informed as to the progress of the sale.

Bidding for a property

The lots will be offered and the bidding taken to the highest possible level and once the gavel falls, the contracts will be exchanged. The buyer purchases the property at the price they bid - this cannot be negotiated and the stipulated terms cannot be changed. The buyer will then pay 10% of the purchase price on the day and completion occur 28 days later. The funds are then paid to the seller less the fees of the Auctioneers and those of the seller's solicitor.

The atmosphere of an auction room can be extremely exciting and competitive and it is often the case that an interested party will bid in excess of the figure that had previously been set as their maximum. In some cases, the prices achieved at auction can be higher than those achieved by private treaty.

The seller will provide a legal pack that may be inspected at any time. Auctioneers will strongly advise that professional advice is obtained from a legal representative. Details of the seller's solicitors will be available and, should a mortgage be required, it is advisable to have this in place prior to the sale. Again, Auctioneers strongly advise that funding is discussed with a professional advisor prior to attending the sale.

The successful buyer will be required to pay 10% of the purchase price on the day, together with a buyer's premium which is normally £250 including VAT.

The balance of the purchase price is required on the agreed completion day and this is normally 28 days after the auction, however this can vary so best to check with the auction house.

How do prospective purchasers find out legal and survey information for the properties in which they are interested?

A legal pack is requested from each of the vendor's solicitors and this contains copies of all legal papers, which will be required by any prospective purchasers for them to make an informed decision regarding the purchase of any lot.

The pack will include office copy entries and plans, the relevant local authority search, leases (if applicable), Special Conditions of Sale, replies to pre-contract enquiries and any other relevant documents. A copy of these legal packs can usually be obtained from auctioneers for a small charge. Should any additional information be required, the seller's solicitors are listed in the catalogue and can be contacted directly. All legal packs are available for inspection at each auction.

Any purchase at auction takes place under the assumption that documentation and the terms of the contract have been read.

It is strongly recommended that any potential purchasers carry out full investigations for any lot in which they have an interest and a survey is an integral part of that investigation.

How is finance arranged?

Should a mortgage be required, approval in principle must be obtained prior to auction. Lenders are now familiar with the auction process and are usually willing to provide a mortgage offer for buyers intending to purchase at auction. A valuation and survey will be required along with legal evidence that there are no issues that will affect the value.

It is essential that the lender can provide funds within the timescale for completion. On the day of the auction, the purchaser will need to pay 10% of the purchase price and must ensure there are cleared funds to pay this amount. Sometimes, finance can be arranged through an Auctioneers on request.

Can lots be bought before auction?

Vendors may consider offers submitted before auction day. Any such offers need to be submitted in writing to an Auctioneers - this will be referred to the vendor and their instruction will be passed on to the prospective purchaser. Any offers will have to be unconditional and the buyer must be in a position to exchange contracts and pay the required deposit before auction day. With most auctioneers, no offers are considered within five days of the auction.

What should I take with me to the auction room?

The items required are as follows:

- Deposit cheque or banker's draft for any potential purchase
- Identification - this is legally required under the money laundering regulations. Therefore a driving licence or passport is required and a current utility bill to show proof of residence.
- Details of solicitors acting on behalf of any potential purchaser.

What happens if a prospective purchaser is unable to attend the auction?

If prospective purchasers are unable to attend the sale, it is possible to bid in other ways:

- By telephone - the interested party will be telephoned as the lot is being auctioned.
- By proxy in writing - a member of the auction team will represent the buyer, who has previously specified their maximum bid

In each case a registration form and cheque to cover the deposit and buyer's fee, are required prior to the date of the auction. A bidder's registration form is printed in the catalogue or alternatively can be obtained from the office

Will the property be insured when I purchase?

No - the purchaser at auction is responsible for obtaining Building insurance cover from the moment the property is deemed sold to them at auction.

Sale by tender

As an alternative to auction, sale by tender is like a blind auction; you don't know what the other potential buyers are offering. A form of tender is included in the sales details and sometimes sets out the contract details. Always check these details with your conveyancer, because often you cannot pull out after the offer is accepted.

Buyers put their offers in an envelope, sometimes with a 10%

deposit. These must be received by the seller's agent at a specified date, at which time the seller will accept one of the offers.

Sale by tender is sometimes used when there have been two or three offers at similar prices.

House swapping

House swapping is an unorthodox but cost effective way of obtaining the property that you are looking for. It is a very efficient way of buying a property. Essentially, you find the property that you want and the seller moves into your house. There is no chain because you are cutting out other buyers. Obviously, the biggest problem is finding someone that you want to swap with and who wants to swap with you.

In practice, the estate agent should be the ideal key player in any swap arrangement. They have a large number of people on their books and who have provided details of their requirements. However, this way of operating seems to be beyond all but the most enterprising estate agencies. In practice, most swaps happen through coincidence.

Saving money through swapping homes

There is a significant saving to be made by swapping homes. If you are the one trading down, for example you have a home worth £275,000 and you want to swap it for a flat worth £150,000, the owner of the flat will be paying for your house with part cash part property. As far as HMRC is concerned this is not a sale on which you would pay stamp duty, but a transfer on which you would pay a notional sum of just £5. However, in this particular type of transaction solicitors must draw up the deal as a single contract with the more expensive property paid partly in kind and partly in cash. You can also save on estate agents fees if you find your swap independently. A useful website dealing with home swaps is:

www.home-swap.org.uk. Registration on the site is free.

Now read the key points from Chapter 3.

****

Key Points From Chapter Three

1   Give careful thought to all the costs of buying property.

2   Some banks lend up to 95% of the purchase price of a property. However, in these straitened times banks are reluctant to lend too much. The more that you lend the more that it costs.

3   If the house or flat costs over £125,000 stamp duty will be payable.

4   You should consider very carefully the need for a full structural survey when buying a property.

5   Always bargain, never offer the asking price.

4

More About Mortgages

Most people purchasing a property will need a mortgage. There are many products on the market and deposits are not always required. However, it is crucial that you are in possession of all the facts when making a decision about a mortgage.

Financial advisers will give you plenty of advice but not always the best advice. Sometimes it is better to go to the lender direct. Before you talk to lenders, work out what your priorities are, such as tax advantage, early repayment and so on. Make sure that you are aware of the costs of life cover.

Lenders-Banks and building societies

There is little or no difference between the mortgages offered by banks and building societies. Because banks borrow against the wholesale money markets, the interest rate they charge to borrowers will fluctuate (unless fixed) as and when their base rate changes. Building societies however, which will rely more heavily on their savers deposits to fund their lending, may adjust the interest rate charged for variable mortgages only once a year. This may be a benefit or disadvantage, depending on whether rates are going up or down.

Centralised lenders

Centralised lenders borrow from the money markets to fund their lending and have no need for the branch network operated by banks and building societies. Centralised lenders, which came to the fore during the 1980s, particularly the house price boom, have been criticised for being quick to implement increases but slow to implement decreases, through rate reductions. This is, simply, because they exist to make profit. Therefore, you should be cautious indeed before embarking on a mortgage with lenders of this kind.

Brokers and "independent" financial advisors

Brokers act as intermediaries between potential borrowers and mortgage providers. If they are "tied" agents they can only advise on the products of one bank, insurance company or building society. If they are independent they should, technically, advise and recommend on every product in the market place.

A word of warning. It is up to you to ask detailed questions about any product a broker offers you. Since 2013, advisors have to charge a fee and advertise this fee. prior to this they charged a commission, the costs of which fell onto the borrower. Many brokers sell unsuitable products because they receive healthy commissions. In the 1980s it became impossible to enter an estate agents without being forced to enter into discussions with financial advisers who were intent on selling you products which made them a lot of money. If possible, you should arrange a mortgage direct with a bank and avoid so called independent brokers.

How much can you borrow?

There is a standard calculation for working out the maximum mortgage that you will be allowed. For one borrower, three times annual salary, for a joint mortgage, two or two and a half times combined. Lenders, however, will vary and some will lend more. Be very careful not to overstretch yourself. As stated, banks and building societies have tightened up their lending criteria and mortgages are hard to obtain without hefty deposits. The Financial Conduct Authority have introduced tough new rules to ensure that no one can borrow more than they can afford to repay. These rules represent a further tightening up after the fiasco of the last ten years which has ultimately led to the present crisis. Under the new rules, interest only mortgages will only be offered to people with a firm and clear repayment plan, rather than simply relying on the rise in house prices to cover repayment of the capital. Lenders will also have to take account of future interest rate increases on repayment costs.

Mortgage Market Review

New rules came into force in April 2014 means that those seeking a mortgage should brace themselves for a long wait to see a mortgage adviser, three-hour interviews at the bank and forensic analysis of your daily spending habits.

Even after jumping through all those hoops, success is not guaranteed – experts have warned thousands of buyers and home owners are likely to be rejected because they do not meet the new requirements.

The City regulator, the Financial Conduct Authority (FCA), has introduced the new rules, known as the Mortgage Market Review, to ensure borrowers are issued with mortgages they can afford both now and in the future. The FCA was concerned that lenders were making it too easy to get a mortgage before the financial crisis. Many households borrowed too much money and found they were unable to keep up their repayments when the financial crisis struck.

So-called "self-cert" loans, where borrowers declared their income but did not have to prove or "certify" it, were common and people routinely exaggerated earnings to borrow more. Interest-only loans also caused problems. Borrowers flocked to these deals because their monthly repayments were lower, but they had no way to repay the capital at the end of the loan.

To ensure safer lending in future, mortgage providers are now responsible for assessing whether customers can afford the loan in the long term. This includes buyers and those who are remortgaging and want to increase the size of the loan, vary the time frame or transfer it to a new property.

Deposits

Most banks and building societies used to lend 95% maximum, some more than that. However, for now those days are over. Lenders will usually require higher deposits. The best source of information for reputable lenders is in the weekend newspapers. However, still, the more that you put down the better deal that you are likely to get from the lender.

Help to Buy Scheme
To be eligible for help from Help to Buy, you must:

-Have a deposit of at least 5%;
-Be looking to buy a home worth £600,000 or less;
-Be purchasing a property you intend to live in most of the time;
-This means you can't buy a property you intend to let out or use as a second home.

There are two parts to the scheme - equity loans and mortgage guarantees

Help to Buy scheme - mortgage guarantees

Most of the UK's biggest mortgage lenders have signed up to offer Help to Buy mortgages, as well as smaller lenders.
Help to Buy mortgages work like this:

-You'll put down a deposit of at least 5%
-You can borrow up to 95% of the property's price from a mortgage lender.
-The government will then guarantee any mortgage borrowing above 80% of the property's value.

For example, if you took out a 85% mortgage the government would guarantee to repay your lender up to 10% of its value if you defaulted.

But all of this goes on behind the scenes, for you as the borrower it is no different to any other mortgage. You are responsible for repaying the whole loan and could face repossession if you fell into arrears.

For the lender, this will mean that lending to people with small deposits will carry much less risk, so it should create much more choice for borrowers. However the government is giving lenders the freedom to set their own interest rates as part of the scheme, so there are no guarantees you'll get an attractive rate.

How equity loans work

A Help to Buy equity loans are only available to people who want to buy a new build property. They work like this:

The government lends you up to 20% of the property's value as an equity loan;

-You'll need a deposit of at least 5%;
-You'll need to get a mortgage of 75% of the property's value.

So if you wanted to buy a house worth £200,000, it would break down as:

-A £40,000 loan from the government;
-A £10,000 deposit put down by you;
-A £150,000 from a mortgage lender.

The benefit to getting an equity loan from the government is that with a larger amount to put down, you'll hopefully get a better mortgage rate from your lender.

Equity loans - what you'll have to pay back

-The equity loan is interest free for the first five years;
-From the sixth year onwards you will pay an admin fee;
-The admin fee will start at 1.75% of the loan;#
-The admin fee will increase every year by any increase in the Retail Prices Index plus 1%.

Remember, you will be paying these fees in addition to your mortgage repayments and the equity loan from the government will not be decreasing in size (unless you opt to repay part of it early). So, over time the cost of the admin fee could become pretty expensive.

You will need to repay the equity loan in full after 25 years, when your mortgage term finishes or when you sell your home - whichever happens first. You will repay the market value of the loan at the time, rather than a fixed cash amount. In practice, this means:

-You take a 20% equity loan to buy a property worth £200,000, or £40,000;
-When you sell the property, it's worth £250,000;
-You repay £50,000 - this is 20% of the new value of your home, not the amount you borrowed;
-If the property had dropped in value, you'd pay less than you borrowed.

You can also choose to repay part of the loan early in chunks of either 10% or 20% of the total value.

Joint mortgages

If you want a joint mortgage, as for any other shared loan you and your partner have a shared responsibility for ensuring that the necessary repayments are made. If something happens to one partner then the other has total responsibility for the loan.

Main types of mortgage
Endowment

With this type of mortgage, you have to take out an endowment insurance policy which is then used to pay off the mortgage loan in a lump sum at the end of the term. There are a number of different types designed to achieve the same end:

- Low cost with profits. This is the usual sort of endowment, guaranteeing to pay back part of the loan only. However, because bonuses are likely to be added, it is usually enough to pay off the loan in full;

- Unit linked endowment. With this, the monthly premiums are used to buy units in investment funds. The drawback is that there is no guarantee how much the policy will be worth on maturity, since this depends on how well the investments have performed.

A word of warning. Endowment products were pushed heavily by financial brokers. There was an obsession with them in the 1980's. This is because they earn big commission for those people that sell them. Like a lot of salespeople, motivated by greed salespeople, some advisers failed to reveal the down side.

This is:

-Endowments are investment linked and there is no guarantee that they will have matured sufficiently at the end of the term to repay the mortgage. This leaves you in a mess. A repayment mortgage will definitely have paid off the mortgage at the end of the term. If you change your mortgage and decide that you do not wish to continue with an endowment mortgage, and so cash in the policy early you will almost certainly get a poor return unless it is close to maturity. In the early years of the policy, most of your payments will go towards administration and commission (a fact that your broker does not always reveal). The alternative in these circumstances is to maintain the endowment until it matures, treating it as a stand-alone investment which will, hopefully, make you some money eventually.

Repayment mortgages

This mortgage, where the borrower makes regular repayments to pay the mortgage off over the term is a fairly safe bet. However, if you plan to move house every five years then this will not necessarily be the best mortgage for you. With a repayment mortgage, you pay interest every month but only a small proportion of the capital, particularly in the early years of the mortgage. An endowment mortgage, while more risky, could be better for you under these circumstances, since you can transfer the plan from property to property, while it can, hopefully, grow steadily as it matures.

Pension mortgages

Similar to the other products except that the payments go into a personal pension plan with the remainder after paying the mortgage forming the basis of a pension. The same characteristics apply as to the others.

Interest only mortgage

The borrower pays interest only on the loan, and decides how he or she will pay the loan off at the end. The lender will want to know this too, particularly in the light of the new rules being introduced, mentioned above.

Mixed mortgages

A new development is that one or two lenders now allow borrowers to mix a combination of mortgages in one deal, customising the mortgage to suit each individual.

Foreign currency mortgages

Some foreign banks offer short-term mortgages in the foreign currency of that bank. Their lending criteria can be much more relaxed than trying to borrow from a British lender. The advantage of this sort of mortgage depends on currency fluctuations. If the pound is stable or rises, the borrower benefits. If the pound drops, the borrower will have to pay more. These types of home loans should be left to more sophisticated investors as there is the potential to get into trouble unless you have a clear grasp on the implications of such a mortgage.

Cashbacks

You probably saw the adverts offering large sums of cashback if you took a particular product. If you read the small print, unless you took the highest mortgage available with the highest deposit then you would not get anywhere near such a sum. This mortgage was typical of the many mortgages on offer in the pre-credit crunch times. You would be very hard pushed to see such an offer now.

What to do if you feel that you have been given wrong advice

The mortgage lending market is very complicated and many people have suffered at the hands of financial advisors and others who have given incorrect advice. Mortgage regulation has not been very tight. However, the basic framework is as follows:

- Sales of mortgage linked investments like endowments or pensions are regulated by the Financial Conduct Authority. Anyone selling investments must be qualified and registered and must be able to clearly demonstrate that the policy that they have recommended is suitable. All registered individuals and firms are inspected by regulators and can be fined or expelled from the industry if guilty of wrongly selling products.

- By contrast, information on mortgages is currently regulated by the industry only, voluntarily, under a code of mortgage practice sponsored by the Council of Mortgage Lenders. Although most of the big players are signed up to the code there are still some who are not. Check first before taking advice.

How to complain

- Complain first to the company that sold you the product, going through its internal complaints procedure.
- If you are unhappy with the firm's decision, approach the relevant complaints body. For mortgage advisors employed directly by lenders, or complaints about lenders generally, contact the Financial Ombudsman Service on 0300 123 9 123 or www.financial-ombudsman.org.uk
- For mortgage lenders which are not building societies or banks but which are signed up to the mortgage code, the Chartered Institute of Arbitrators 020 7421 7455 www.ciarb.org will assist.
- If your complaint is about a mortgage broker, contact the Chartered Institute of Arbitrators which may be able to help if the firm is registered under the code.
- Complaints about endowments, pensions and other investments is handled by the Financial Conduct Authority 0800 111 67 68 www.fca..org.uk and are dealt with by the financial ombudsman Service.

The most common complaint is to do with endowments. A lot of people bought products which they came to regret. They are a major source of profit to the provider-and all those in between-but the person left holding the problem is the consumer.

If you believe that you have been given bad advice about anything to do with the insurance or investment side of a product then you should approach the Financial Services Authority.

The Building Society Association or the British Bankers Association have free publications that should help you. In addition, the Consumers Association, "Which" runs regular articles on mortgages. Remember - always ask questions. Never rush into anything. Always take advice if you are uncertain. Banks and building societies themselves are usually a better source, a safer source than individual advisers.

Borrowing and the internet

Almost all lenders have their own sites and many operate internet only loans with keener rates than those available on the high street. But there are also growing numbers of mortgage broker sites, offering mortgage calculators so that you can work out how much you can afford to borrow and how much the true cost of your loan will be. The following are a selection of independent sites:

www.moneysupermarket.co.uk
This is an online mortgage broker with a choice of over 4000 variable, fixed rate, capped and discounted mortgages as well as more specialist loans for right to buy, buy to let and self build property, also self certification loans.

www.moneynet.co.uk
This is an independent on line mortgage broker, offering mortgages

from over 100 lenders. Again, as with all these sites it will provide a clear and comprehensive picture of mortgages available and is easy to use, just follow the instructions.

www.moneyextra.co.uk

An independent financial advisor with access to over 4500 products including all kinds of mortgages for all types of client.

Now read the Key Points from Chapter Four overleaf.

****

Key Points From Chapter Four

1   There are many mortgage products on the market. Choose carefully. Understand advice- make sure all is clear.

2   The more you borrow, the more you pay at the outset and over the term.

3   If you are given wrong advice or feel aggrieved in any way there are mechanisms for complaint.

5

Selling Your Home

_____

Estate agents

Ask for quotes from at least three agents before instructing one or more of them. The fee is normally based on the selling price of the house and is between 1 - 3 per cent of the final selling price. However, VAT (currently 20%) will be added on to this. The next chapter on conveyancing gives an idea of the processes involved once a buyer is found.

DIY Selling

If you want to save the cost of instructing an agent to sell your house, you could try to sell it yourself. Around 4 - 5% of homes in the UK are sold privately. There are a number of useful guides which are dedicated to this subject. One site worth visiting is www. uknetguide.co.uk.

Setting the price if selling yourself

You need to see how much similar properties are sold for in the area. If this proves difficult, get a professional valuation. See Yellow Pages under Surveyors or Valuers or contact the Royal Institution of Chartered Surveyors. A valuation report will only value and will not assess structural soundness. A survey is needed for that. Put together the sales particulars in the same way that an estate agent would. It is advisable to put a disclaimer on these details such as "these particulars are believed to be accurate and are set out as a general outline only for the guidance of interested buyers. They do not constitute, nor constitute parts of, an offer or contract.

Advertising your property independently

There are a number of ways you can advertise your property. Local papers will advertise for you and also there are free ad papers. In addition, there are a number of companies with a computerised sales network who will charge you a flat fee for advertising. Be accurate with the details - you may leave yourself open to damages through misrepresentation. If an offer is made to you then you should then hand matters over to your solicitor.

As discussed, some sellers handle their own conveyancing lock stock and barrel. This includes the legal side. However, this book cannot advise you on legal conveyancing. That is a separate matter. Suffice to say that it follows a standard format. It is easier, in the light of the reduced prices available to appoint a solicitor to do this side for you.

Selling at Auction

Advantages of auction

In chapter 3, we looked at buying properties at auction. here are a few tips for you when selling a property at auction. An auction is an efficient and cost effective way of selling property and if prepared properly with intensive marketing, advertising and mailing, will result in the greatest possible exposure of the lots offered. To maximize the effectiveness of the marketing, considerable thought must be given to the guide price, which needs to be tailored to generate competitive bidding in the auction room, thus ensuring that the best price is being achieved. Although some properties are more suitable for sale by private treaty, taking this route does present uncertainties over terms such as sale price and timing of exchange and completion.

Selling by auction however, offers a high degree of certainty that a sale will be achieved on a given day and, significantly, on the fall of the gavel an immediate binding contract is formed. As no further negotiation is permitted the entire sale process, from instruction to exchange of contracts can be, is achieved within as little as six to eight weeks.

For vendors with a large number of properties to sell, auctions provide a highly efficient method of sale allowing for a total or phased disposal programme selling in individual lots thus maximising receipts. For those selling in a fiduciary capacity, there is the added advantage of the sale being entirely open and transparent. Most types of property are suitable for auction provided that a realistic reserve price is agreed.

Who sells at auction?

Auction is now regarded as the optimum method of sale for many sellers who range from private investors and property companies to banks, housing associations and local authorities.

When do you want to sell?

Decide when you want to sell your property and which auction you would like to put it in. Sale dates and venues can be found on auctioneers websites.

What information do auctioneers need?

In order to give you the best possible advice auctioneers will need the following details:

Address
Description
Photograph
Tenure and Tenancy (if applicable) details
Floor plan or site plan
Anything else you consider to be material

Once the auctioneers have received this information, they will provide an estimate of the likely sale price of your property at Auction. Together with a proposed reserve, they shall send you a copy of their standard agency contract setting out their terms and conditions. Once the maximum reserve price is agreed you will be asked to sign and return the standard agency contract to confirm your instructions, at which time the Entry Fee becomes payable.

Proof of identity

If an auctioneer has not sold for you before they will require proof of your identity and address before they can market your property.

How much does it cost? Auction Entry Fee

All auctioneers will charge a fee to enter a property into an auction. This fee is payable whether the property is sold or not. The fee is a contribution towards the cost of marketing and catalogue production.

The fee will depend on how much space is taken in the catalogue for the property.

Commission

In the event of a sale, an auctioneer's commission is up to 2% of the sale price plus VAT for a sole agency or 2.5% plus VAT for a joint agency. A joint agency is usually advisable where the auctioneer feels it is necessary to include a local estate agent to handle local enquiries and conduct viewing. The auction house surveyors will confirm the auction entry fee and commission rate with you in writing before accepting your instructions.

Sales particulars

Once the auctioneer has been formally instructed, the property will be inspected by one of their surveyors, measurements taken where appropriate, and the property will be photographed. Draft sales particulars will then be forwarded to you and to your solicitors for approval and/or amendments.

Legal documents

At the same time your solicitors will be instructed to prepare a legal pack containing special conditions of sale, title documents, leases (where applicable), searches, planning documentation and office copy entries so that they are available to interested parties either by post or on line.

Guide price

The auction team will recommend a guide price which you will need to approve before marketing begins. It is important to set the guide price at a realistic level which is attractive to buyers. This will generate competitive bidding in the auction room and ensure that best value is achieved.

Marketing your property

Marketing will usually start approximately three to four weeks prior to the auction sale. Auction Houses produce thousands of catalogues for each auction. These are sent to prospective buyers such as private investors, property companies and developers.

E-marketing

Catalogues are available online and auctioneers send regular email alerts to the private investors who are registered on the site.

Advertising and PR

Good auctioneers will advertise in the key property publications and place advertisements in local newspapers.

Targeted Marketing

Auction houses also target individuals who have previously expressed an interest in similar properties, as well as adjacent occupiers, local agents, local developers, builders and property companies.

Viewings and Surveys

Potential purchasers may want to view your property during the marketing period and have a survey carried out. You should let the auctioneer know how you would prefer viewings to be arranged and we shall arrange access for buyers. In most cases, vacant properties are open at pre-arranged times for viewing. Details will be printed in the catalogue.

Legal documentation

In conjunction with your solicitors the auction house will supply copy documents to prospective purchaser's solicitors and will keep you constantly updated as to the levels of interest shown.

The reserve price

The auction House will agree a reserve price with you for your property a few days before the auction. This is the level below which they will not be authorised to sell. It is important that this be set at a realistic level.

Auction day
The Fall of the Gavel

On the fall of the Auctioneer's gavel, a binding contract is effected. The successful bidder is required to provide the name, address and telephone number of the purchaser and the purchaser's solicitors. The successful bidder will also be asked to provide a deposit for 10% of the purchase price. Identification of the purchaser is always checked at this stage.

Clearance of all deposit cheques is arranged immediately after the auction.

Exchange of Contracts

The Memorandum of Sale is made up in the room and given to the purchaser to sign. The exchange is overseen by the auction house's solicitor. They will forward the purchaser's signed Memorandum of Sale to your solicitor. Completion will usually, take place 20 working days later. The deposit funds are then paid to you less fees.

What happens if the property does not sell on the day?

If your property fails to reach its reserve in the room, someone may still wish to buy it. You will need to decide whether to accept any offer and advise the auction house accordingly. The property may even be sold in the days or weeks after the sale as we continue to market the property.

Quick Results

The entire process, from instruction to exchange of contracts, can be achieved within as little as six to eight weeks.

Now read the key points from Chapter 5.

****

Key points from Chapter Five

- Ask for quotes from at least three agents before agreeing to sell

- You could try to sell your property yourself. Internet selling is becoming more popular

- It is important to get an accurate valuation before selling

- Selling by auction is one route of sale if your property is proving hard to sell

6

Conveyancing a Property

Conveyancing, or the practice of conveyancing, is about how to transfer the ownership of land and property from one person or organisation to another. Land and property can include freehold property, leasehold property (residential) or can include business leases. *Essentially, the process of conveyancing lays down clear procedures for the conveyancer and also sets out each party's position during the sale or acquisition.*

Before understanding the process of conveyancing, however, it is essential to understand something about the legal forms of ownership of property.

Legal ownership of property

There are two main forms of legal ownership of property in Great Britain. If you are about to embark on the sale or acquisition of a house or flat (or business) then you will be dealing in the main with either freehold or leasehold property.

It is very rare indeed to find other forms of ownership, although the government has introduced a form of ownership called 'common hold' that in essence creates the freehold ownership of flats, with common responsibility for communal areas.

Freehold property

In general, if you own the freehold of a house or a piece of land, then you will be the outright owner with no fixed period of time and no one else to answer to (with the exception of statutory authorities).

There may be registered restrictions on title, which will be discussed later. The property will probably be subject to a mortgage so the only other overriding interest will be that of the bank or the building society. The responsibility for repairs and maintenance and general upkeep will be the freeholders. The law can intervene if certain standards are not maintained. The deed to your house will be known as the "freehold transfer document" which will contain any rights and obligations. Usually, the transfer document will list any "encumbrances" (restrictions) on the use of the land, such as rights of way of other parties, sales restrictions etc. The deeds to your home are the most important documentation. As we will see later, without deeds and historical data, such as the root of title, it can be rather complicated selling property. This is why the system of land registration in use in this country has greatly simplified property transactions.

Any person owning freehold property is free to create another interest in land, such as a lease or a weekly or monthly tenancy, subject to any restrictions the transfer may contain.

Leasehold property

If a person lives in a property owned by someone else and has an agreement for a period of time, usually a long period, over 21 years and up to 99 years or 125 years, in some cases 999 years, then they are a leaseholder.

The conveyancing of leasehold property is, potentially, far more problematic than freehold property, particularly when the flat is in a block with a number of units. The lease is a contract between landlord and tenant which lays down the rights and obligations of both parties and should be read thoroughly by both the leaseholder and, in particular, the conveyancer. Once signed then the purchaser is bound by all the clauses in the contract. It is worth taking a little time looking at the nature of a lease before discussing the rather more complex process of conveyancing. Again, it has to be stated that it is of the utmost importance that both the purchaser and the vendor understand the nature of a lease.

The lease
Preamble

The start of a lease is called the preamble. This defines the landlord and purchaser and also the nature of the property in question (the demise). It will also detail the remaining period of the lease.

Leaseholders covenants

Covenants are best understood as obligations and responsibilities. Leaseholder's covenants are therefore a list of things that leaseholders should do, such as pay their service charges and keep the interior of the dwelling in good repair and not to, for example, alter the structure. The landlord's covenants will set out the obligations of the landlord, which is usually to maintain the structure and exterior of the block, light common parts etc.

One unifying theme of all leasehold property is that, notwithstanding the landlord's responsibilities, it is the leaseholder who will pay for everything out of a service charge.

Leases will make detailed provisions for the setting, managing and charging of service charges, which should include a section on accounting. All landlords of leaseholders are accountable under the

83

Landlord and Tenant Act 1985, as amended. These Acts will regulate the way a landlord treats a leaseholder in the charging and accounting of service charges.

In addition, the 1996 Housing Act, as amended by the 2002 Commonhold and Leasehold Reform Act has provided further legislation protecting leaseholders by introducing the right of leaseholders to go to Leasehold Valuation Tribunals if they are unhappy with levels and management of charges and also to carry out audits of charges. It is vital that, when buying a leasehold property that you read the lease. Leases tend to be different from each other and nothing can be assumed. When you buy a property, ensure that the person selling has paid all debts and has contributed to some form of "sinking fund" whereby provision has been built up for major repairs in the future. Make sure that you will not be landed with big bills after moving in and that, if you are, there is money to deal with them. After a lease has been signed then there is little or no recourse to recoup any money owed.

These are all the finer points of leases and the conveyancer has to be very vigilant. In particular read the schedules to the lease as these sometimes contain rather more detail.

One of the main differences between leasehold and freehold property is that the lease is a long tenancy agreement which contains provisions which give the landlord rather a lot of power to manage (or mismanage) and it is always a possibility that a leaseholder can be forced to give up his or her home in the event of non compliance with the terms of the lease. This is known as forfeiture.

Under legislation referred to earlier, a new 'no fault right to manage' has been introduced. This enables leaseholders who are unhappy with the management of their property, to take over the management with relative ease. The Act applies to most landlords, with the exception of Local Authorities. These powers go a long way to curb the excesses or inefficiencies of numerous landlords and provide more control and greater security for leaseholders.

Check points

There are key areas of a lease that should be checked when purchasing. Some have already been discussed.

- What is the term left on the lease?
- Is the preamble clear, i.e. is the area which details landlord, tenant and demised (sold) premises, clear?
- Is the lease assignable- i.e. can you pass on the lease without landlords permission or does it need surrendering at sale or a license to assign?
- What is the ground rent and how frequently will you pay it?
- What is the level of service charge, if any, and how is it collected, apportioned, managed and accounted for?
- What are the general restrictions in the lease, can you have pets for example, can you park cars and do you have a designated space?
- What are the respective repairing obligations? As we have seen, the leaseholder will pay anyway but the landlord and leaseholder will hold respective responsibilities. This is an important point because occasionally, there is no stated responsibility for upkeep and the environment deteriorates as a consequence, diminishing the value of the property.

Two systems of conveyancing

After gaining an understanding of the nature of the interest in land that you are buying, it is absolutely essential to understand the two systems of conveyancing property in existence, as this will determine, not so much the procedure because the initial basic steps in conveyancing, such as carrying out searches, are common to both forms of land, registered and unregistered, but the way you go about the process and the final registration.

Registered and unregistered land

In England and Wales the method of conveyancing to be used in each particular transaction very much depends on whether the land is *registered* or *unregistered* land. If the title, or proof of ownership, of land and property has been registered under the Land Registration Acts 1925-86 then the Land Registry (see below) will be able to furnish the would-be conveyancer with such documentation as is required to establish ownership, third party rights etc. If the land has not been registered then proof of ownership of the land in question must be traced through the title deeds.

Registered land

As more and more conveyancing is falling within the remit of the Land Registry, because it is compulsory to register land throughout England and Wales, it is worth outlining this system briefly at this stage.

The Land Registration Acts of 1925 established the Land Registry (HM Land Registry). The Land Registry is a department of the Civil Service, at its head is the Chief Land Registrar. All applications to the Land Registry must be made within the district in question.

There is a specific terminology in use within conveyancing, particularly within the land registry:

a) *a piece of land*, or parcel of land is known as a *registered title*
b) the owner of land is referred to as the *registered proprietor*

c) a conveyance of registered land is called *a transfer*

d) a transaction involving registered land is known as *a dealing*

The main difference between the two types of conveyancing *registered* and *unregistered* concerns what is known *as proof of title*. In the case of land that is unregistered the owner will prove title by showing the would-be purchaser the documentary evidence which shows how he or she came to own the land and property.

In the case of registered land the owner has to show simply that he or she is registered at the Land Registry as the registered proprietor. Proof of registration is proof of ownership, which is unequivocal. In registered land the documents proving ownership are replaced by the fact of registration. Each separate title or ownership of land has a title number, which the Land Registry uses to trace ownership, or confirm ownership. The description of each title on the register is identified by the *title number,* described by reference to the filed plan (indicating limits and extent of ownership). With registered conveyancing the Land Registry keeps the register of title and file plan and title. The owner (proprietor) is issued with a Land Certificate. If the land in question is subject to a mortgage then the mortgagee is issued with a Land Certificate.

Production of the Land Certificate

With registered land, whenever there is a sale, or disposition, then the Land Certificate must be produced to the Land Registry in the appropriate district. If proved that a Certificate is lost or destroyed then a new one can be issued by the Land Registry.

The key steps in the process of conveyancing property

Before the buyer exchanges contracts on a property, whether registered or unregistered, and then completes the purchase a number of searches are always carried out. These are:

Enquiry's before contract
Local land charges search
Enquiry's of the local authority
Index map search
The above searches will now be carried out by the seller, or by the agent acting for the seller, prior to marketing the property through the HIP.

These are the most essential and common searches.

Making enquiry's before contract
These are enquiry's to the seller, or the Vendor of the property and are aimed at revealing certain facts about the property that the seller has no legal obligation to disclose to the buyer. There are certain matters, which are always raised. These are:

a) Whether there are any existing boundary disputes
b) What services are supplied to the property, whether electricity, gas or other
c) Any easements or covenants in the lease. These are stipulations in the lease, which give other certain rights, such as rights of way.
d) Any guarantees in existence
Planning considerations
a) Adverse rights affecting the property
b) Any fixtures and fittings

c) Whether there has been any breach of restriction affecting the property

If the property is newly built, information will be required concerning any outstanding works or future guarantees of remedying defects. Where a property is leasehold, information will be required about the lessor.

Registered conveyancers will use a standard form to raise these enquiry's, so that the initial search is exhaustive. As part of the move towards openness in the process of buying and selling property, and also an attempt to speed up the process of sale, the Law Society has introduced new forms which the solicitor, or buyer if carrying out his or her own conveyancing, is being encouraged to use. These are Seller's Property Information Forms relating to freehold and leasehold property, that the seller and solicitor will respectively fill in, a form relating to fixtures, fittings and contents and a form relating to complete information and requisitions on title.

These forms can be obtained from a legal stationers, such as Oyez and have the pre-fix Prop 1-7.

If a conveyancer is being used then it is advisable to ask whether or not they are using these newly introduced forms. The main point is that you should think long and hard about the type of questions that should be raised. The vendor does not have to answer the questions, but beware a vendor who refuses to disclose answers. Answers given by the vendor do not form part of the subsequent contract and therefore cannot be used against that person in the event of future problems. However, the Misrepresentations Act of 1976 could be evoked if a deliberate misrepresentation has caused problems.

Local land charges search

The Local Land Charges Act 1975 requires District Councils, London Borough Councils and the City of London Corporation to maintain a Local Land Charges Registry for the area. Local land charges can be divided into two areas:

a) Financial charges on the land for work carried out by the local authority
b) restrictions on the use of land

The register is further divided into twelve parts:

a) general financial charges
b) specific financial charges
c) planning charges
d) miscellaneous charges and provisions
e) charges for improvements of ways over fenland
f) land compensation charges
g) new town charges
h) civil aviation charges
i) open cast coal mining charges
j) listed buildings charges
k) light obstruction notices
l) drainage scheme charges

All charges are enforceable by the local authority except g and i, which are enforced by statutory bodies and private individuals generally. A buyer should search in all parts of this particular register and this can be done by a personal or official search. A personal search, as the name suggests, involves the individual or their agent attending at the local authority office and, on paying the relevant fee, personally searching the register. The charges are registered against the land concerned and not against the owner. The official search is the one most favored because, in the event of missing a vital piece of information the chances of compensation are far higher than with a personal search.

With the official search a requisition for a search and for an official certificate of search is sent to the Registrar of Local Land Charges for the area within which the land is situated. There is a fee and the search is carried out by the Registrars staff, which results in a certificate being sent to the person making the request, which clearly outlines any charges. The Registrar may require a plan of the land as well as the postal address. Separate searches are made of each parcel of land being purchased.

Local authority searches

There is a standard form in use for these particular types of searches. This is known as "Con 29 England and Wales" Revised April 2000, with the format of the form differing slightly for inner London boroughs. Any of the forms in the process can be obtained from legal stationers.

The standard forms in use contain a statement to the effect that the local authority is not responsible for errors unless negligence is proved. Many of the enquiries relate specifically to planning matters, whilst other elements of the search are concerned about roads and whether they are adopted and whether there are likely to be any costs falling onto property owners.

We will be considering planning matters concerning the individual property a little later. Other enquiry's relate to possible construction of new roads which may affect the property, the location of sewers and pipes and whether the property is in an area of compulsory registration of title, a smoke control area or slum clearance area. The form used is so constructed that part 2 of the form contains questions, which must be initialled by the purchaser before they are answered. Again these questions cover planning and other matters.

Other enquiry's can be asked by the individual, which are answered at the authorities discretion. In addition to the above, which are the major searches, there are others that the conveyancer has to be aware of. These are as follows:

Searches in the Index map and parcels index of the Land register

If the land has been registered the title will be disclosed and whether it is registered leasehold or freehold. Registered rent charges are also disclosed by the search. (See chapter 7.)

Commons Registration Act (1965) search

This act imposes a duty on County Councils to keep a register relating to village greens and common land and interests over them, such as right of way.

Coal mining search

The request for this search if relevant, is designed to reveal the whereabouts of mineshafts and should be sent to the local Area Coal Board office, or its equivalent. The search will disclose past workings and any subsidence, proposed future workings and the proximity of opencast workings. It is usually well known if there is a problem, or potential problem with coal mining in an area and this search is essential if that is the case.

Other enquiry's

There are a number of other bodies from which it might be appropriate to request a search. These include British Rail, statutory undertakers such as electricity and gas boards, planning authorities generally, rent assessment committees and so on. These will only usually be necessary if there is a direct link between the property being purchased and a particular circumstance within an area or property.

Planning matters relating to specific properties

It is obviously very necessary to determine whether or not any illegal alterations have been carried out to the property you wish to purchase, before reaching the point of exchange of contracts. This is to ensure that the vendor has complied with relevant planning legislation, if any material changes have been made, and that you will not be required at a later date to carry out remedial work. The Local Authority maintains a register of planning applications relating to properties within their boundaries. In addition, the register will also reveal any planning enforcement notices in force against a particular property.

Questions such as these, and also any questions relating to the effect of Structure or Local plans, (specific plans relating to local and borough wide plans for the future) should be made in writing to the local authority or an individual search can be carried out. Usually they are carried out if there is any suspicion that planning regulations may have been breached.

In addition, there may be other considerations, such as whether the building is listed or whether tree preservation orders relating to trees within the cartilage of the property are in force. It is certainly essential to know about these. It is highly recommended that all of these searches are carried out and completed before contracts are exchanged.

The contract for sale

As with many other transactions, a sale of land is effected through a contract. However, a contract, which deals with the sale of land, is governed by the requirements of the Law of Property (miscellaneous provisions) Act 1989, the equitable doctrine of specific performance and the duty of the vendor to provide title to the property.

The Law of Property Act (Miscellaneous provisions) 1988 provides that contracts dealing with the sale of land after 26th September 1989 must be in writing. The contract must contain all the terms and agreements to which the respective parties to the transaction have agreed. The provisions of the Act do not apply to sales at a public auction, contracts to grant a short lease and contracts regulated under the Financial Services Act 1986. If the person purchasing is doing so through an agent then the agent must have authority to act on behalf of the purchaser. Examples of agents are auctioneers and solicitors, also estate agents. If the phrase "subject to contract" is used in a sale then the intention of both parties to the contract is that neither are contractually bound until a formal contract has been agreed by the parties, signed and exchanged.

Therefore, the words "subject to contract" are a protective device, although it is not good to depend on the use of these words throughout a transaction

Procedures in the formation of contract

The vendor's solicitor will usually draw up an initial contract of sale. This is because only this person has access to all the necessary initial documents to begin to effect a contract. The draft contract is prepared in two parts and sent to the purchaser's solicitor (if using a solicitor), the other side will approve or amend the contract as necessary. Both sides must agree to any proposed amendments. After agreement has been reached, the vendor's solicitor will retain one copy of the contract and send the other copy to the solicitor or person acting for the other side. The next stage is for the vendors solicitor to engross (sign and formalise) the contract in two parts. Both parts are then sent to the purchaser's solicitor or other agent who checks that they are correct then sends one part back to the vendor's solicitor.

The Contents of a contract

A contract will be in two parts, *the particulars of sale* and the *conditions of sale.* The particulars of sale give a physical description of the land and also of the interest, which is being sold. A property must be described accurately and a plan may be attached to the contract to emphasize or illustrate what is in the contract. The particulars will also outline whether the property is freehold or leasehold and what kind of lease the vendor is assigning, i.e., head lease (where vendor is owner of the freehold) or underlease, where the vendor is not.

It is very important to determine what kind of lease it is that is being assigned, indeed whether it is assignable or whether permission is needed from the landlord and it is recommended that a solicitor handle this transaction. This is because any purchaser of a lease can find his or her interest jeopardized by the nature of the lease. Where a sub-lease, or under lease is being purchased, the purchasers interest can be forfeited by the actions of the head lessee, the actions of this person being out of control of the purchaser.

Rights, such as easements and also restrictive covenants, which are for the benefit of the land, should be expressly referred to in the particulars of sale. In addition, the vendor should refer to any latent defects affecting his or her property, if known. This includes any encumbrances, which may affect the property.

Misdescription

If the property in the particulars of sale is described wrongly, i.e. there is a mis-statement of fact, such as describing leasehold as freehold land, calling an under-lease a lease or leaving out something that misleads the buyer, in other words, if the misdescription is material, then the purchaser is entitled to rescind the contract. Essentially the contract must describe what is being sold and if it does not, and the buyer is mislead then the contract is inaccurate. If the misdescription is immaterial and insubstantial, and there has been no misrepresentation then the purchaser cannot rescind the contract. However, if the misdescription has affected the purchase price of the property then the purchaser can insist on a reduction in the asking price. The purchaser should claim this compensation before completion takes place. The vendor has no right to rescind the contract if the misdescription is in the purchaser's favour, for example, the area of land sold is greater than that intended. Neither can the vendor compel the purchaser to pay an increased purchase price

Misrepresentation

Misrepresentation is an untrue statement of fact made by one party or his or her agent, which induces the other party to enter into the contract. An opinion and a statement of intention must be distinguished from a statement of fact.

There are three types of misrepresentation, fraudulent misrepresentation, negligent misrepresentation and innocent misrepresentation. Fraudulent misrepresentation is a false statement made knowingly or without belief in its truth, or recklessly. The innocent party may sue through the tort of negligence either before or after the contract is complete and rescind the contract. Negligent misrepresentation, although not fraudulent, is where the vendor or his or her agents cannot prove that the statement they made in relation to the contract was correct.

Remedies available are damages or rescission of the contract. Innocent misrepresentation is where the statement made was neither fraudulently or negligently but is still an untrue statement. Rescission is available for this particular type of misrepresentation. Rescission of contract generally is available under the Misrepresentation Act 1967 s 2(2).

Non-disclosure

Generally, in the law of contract, there is the principle of "caveat emptor" "let the buyer beware". In other words, it is up to the purchaser to ensure that what he or she is buying is worth the money paid for it. Earlier we talked about the importance of searches and also, particularly, the importance of the structural survey. Although the vendor has some responsibility to reveal any defects in the property it is always very advisable for the purchaser to ensure that all checks prior to purchase are carried out thoroughly.

Signing the contract

The vendors solicitor will obtain the vendors signature to the contract, when he is satisfied that the vendor can sell what he is purporting to do through the contract. The purchaser's solicitor or agent will do the same, having checked the replies to all enquiry's before contract. It is also essential to check that a mortgage offer has been made and accepted.

Exchanging contracts

Neither party to the sale is legally bound until there has been an exchange of contracts. At one time, a face to face exchange would have taken place. However, with the rapid increases in property transactions this rarely happen nowadays. Exchange by post is more common. The purchaser will post his or her part of the contract together with the appropriate cheque to cover the agreed deposit, to the purchaser's solicitor or person acting on behalf of that Person. The purchaser's solicitor will usually insert the agreed completion date. On receiving this part of the contract the vendor will add his or her part and send this off in exchange. At this stage, both parties become bound under the contract.

A contract to convey or create an estate in land is registrable as a class C (IV) land charge, an estate contract. You should take further advice on this, as it is not current practice to do so.

Completion

The requirements concerning completion are detailed thoroughly in the general conditions of sale. Payment on completion is one such detail.

Payment on completion should be by one of the following methods:
a) legal tender;
b) bankers draft;
c) an unconditional authority to release any deposit by the stakeholder
d) any other method agreed with the vendor.

At common law, completion takes place whenever the vendor wishes and payment is to be made by legal tender. Also dealt with in the general conditions is failure to complete and notices to complete. Failure to complete can cause difficulty for one of the other parties and the aggrieved party can serve notice on the other to complete by a specific date. The notice has the effect of making "time of the essence" which means that a specific date is attached to completion, after which the contract is discharged.

It is worth mentioning here that it is very advisable indeed to be aware of scams that have been taking place which have cost purchasers dear. This is a sophisticated email scam. Fraudsters are intercepting emails between homebuyers, sellers and their solicitors to target the large sums of money that are exchanged in property transactions. The criminals hijack or spoof the client or solicitors email accounts and provide a bank account into which they instruct funds to be sent. they then drain the money as soon as possible. It can then be very difficult for the purchaser to get the money back.

In the light of this, if you are involved in selling or buying a property, at the point of making any transaction, you should contact the actual firm itself, if necessary going down to see them, to check that all bank account details are correct.

It is always advisable to instruct a solicitor in your home town so that you can readily go to see them if necessary.

Return of pre-contract deposits

The vendor must return any deposit paid to the purchaser if the purchaser drops out before the exchange of contracts. This cannot be prevented and was the subject of a House of Lords ruling.

The position of the parties after exchange of contracts

Once a contract has been exchanged, the purchaser is the beneficial owner of the property, with the vendor owning the property on trust for the purchaser. The vendor is entitled to any rents or other profits from the land during this period, has the right to retain the property until final payments have been made and has a lien (charge/right) over the property in respect of any unpaid purchase monies.

The vendor is bound to take reasonable care of the property and should not let the property fall into disrepair or other damages to be caused during the period between exchange and completion. If completion does not take place at the allotted time and the fault is the purchasers then interest can be charged on the money due.

The purchaser, as beneficial owner of the property is entitled to any increase in the value of the land and buildings but not profits arising. The purchaser has a right of lien over the property, the same as the vendor, in respect of any part of the purchase price paid prior to completion.

Bankruptcy of the vendor

In the unfortunate event of the vendor going bankrupt in between exchange and completion, the normal principles of bankruptcy apply so that the trustee in bankruptcy steps in to the vendor's shoes. The purchaser can be compelled to complete the sale. The trustee in bankruptcy is obliged to complete the sale if the purchaser tenders the purchase money on the completion day.

Bankruptcy of the purchaser

When a purchaser is declared bankrupt in between sale and completion all of his or her property vests in the trustee in bankruptcy. In these circumstances, the vendor can keep any deposit due to him.

Death of Vendor or purchaser

The personal representatives of a deceased vendor can compel the purchaser to sell. The money is conveyed to those representatives who will hold the money in accordance with the terms of any will or in accordance with the rules relating to intestacy if there is no will.

The same position applies to the purchaser's representatives, who can be compelled by the vendor to complete the purchase and who can hold money on the purchaser's behalf.

Now read the key points from chapter 6

****

Key Points From Chapter 6

- Conveyancing is about the practice of transferring a property from one to another.

- There are two main types of property ownership in Britain- Freehold and leasehold

- The lease is the single most important document if buying leasehold

- There are two systems of conveyancing – registered and unregistered.

- The contract of sale must be scrutinised thoroughly before exchange and completion

7

Planning Moving Arrangements

At this stage, you will either have sold your home and /or be ready to move into a new one. The process of moving home is closely linked with the completion of the purchase of another home. That is, assuming that you are moving to another bought property. Of course, you may be moving to a rented home.

However you choose to time your move, there are certain core tasks, as follows:

- Finalise removal and storage arrangements
- Contact electricity/gas/phone/cable companies and any other relevant company to tell them your moving date
- Organise your funds so that you can transfer all remaining money needed to complete the sale into your solicitors account for him/her to pay the sellers solicitor

One main question is: do you get a removal firm or do you do it yourself?

DIY moves

This is cheaper than hiring a removal company, especially if you have a few possessions or no big items of furniture. You will also need willing and able friends. However, do not take the decision to move yourself lightly. Think carefully about the amount of furniture that you have and the fact that your house may be a particularly difficult site to move from.

Using professionals

Professionals know what they are doing and can leave you to organise all the other aspects of moving whilst they do the donkey work. This may cost you more money. However, it may be well worth it. Use a firm which is a member of the British Association of Removers (www.bar.co.uk). Members of this body have to adhere to a code of professional practice, meet minimum standards and provide emergency service and finance guarantees.

Removers can offer various levels of packing services. The most expensive option is for the remover to pack everything. The second most expensive option is for them to pack the breakable things such as glass. The cheapest way is for the removers to provide crates and for you to do your own packing.

If you are going for the professional option:

- Get two or three estimates. You can find the names of local firms through the British Association of Removers, through the yellow pages (www.yell.com) or through Thomson's Directories (www.thomweb.co.uk)
- There are a growing number of websites that include quotes from removal firms (see below)
- You should expect estimators to go through your whole property including gardens and loft
- Check whether your possessions will be covered by your household insurance policy and extend the cover if they are not.

- Don't wait to exchange contracts to organise removers.

The following Websites may be useful:

www.reallymoving.com
This site was launched in 1999 and is the leading provider of online removal services. Registering on the site will get you three quotes from removers. It also covers solicitors, surveyors and others involved in the buying and selling process.

Contacting utilities

A boring but essential task is to contact all of the companies that provide you with services to tell them that you have moved. This should be done after you exchange contracts, obtaining meter readings etc. Most utilities will ask you for confirmation of your new address and moving date in writing. If you cannot face this task then use the following website:

www.iammoving.com

This site was started in 1999 by a consortium of investors and industry figures. The claim is to be the UK's first free online change of address service. You register, enter your old and new address, supply account numbers and meter readings where relevant and iammoving will send the information to the appropriate companies. The process is quick and relatively uncomplicated.

****

8

Buying and Selling in Scotland

Scotland has it own system of law, and buying and selling a house or flat is quite a different process from doing so in England, Wales or Northern Ireland. The system generally works more quickly and there is less risk of gazumping.

Looking for property

Solicitors, property centres and offices. These are the largest source of properties available in Scotland. Often found in town centres, the property centres provide information in a similar way to estate agents outside Scotland.

Newspapers.

Daily Scottish newspapers are a good source of property. Regional and local newspapers carry many details on a regular basis.

Estate agents. These offer the same service

Ownership of property in Scotland

Property in Scotland does not exist as freehold or leasehold, as in England. Instead a "feudal tenure" system exists. This means that, as in freehold, the owner has right to building and land. However, the original owner of the development still has some say over any alterations and use of the land.

These feuing conditions are permanent and should be checked before purchase is considered. A new owner (feuar) can negotiate to have conditions waived, but there may be a charge for this. Further details of the system can be obtained from the lands tribunal for Scotland or your solicitor.

House prices

Property in Scotland is normally sold as "offers over" (sometimes called the upset price) the price set is usually the minimum and may not be negotiated down. This method is used where the property is likely to prove popular and to get the best price. If a quick sale is required a property may be sold as "fixed price" the seller will take the first offer at that price.

If there is more than one prospective purchaser the seller may opt to set a closing date for offers. The process is then like a blind bid, with none of the buyers knowing the price anyone else is bidding. Although the seller usually accepts the highest price, this is not always the case; other factors, such as date of entry, may be taken into consideration.

The buying process
Surveys

These are carried out before a formal offer is made. In some circumstances you may end up losing money, if your offer is not accepted. There are no licensed conveyancers in Scotland. Because solicitors do all the conveyancing and are so involved in the process then they will usually arrange surveys.

Making an offer

Your interest in buying a house is relayed via your solicitor to the selling solicitor by word of mouth. It does not have any legal standing and either party may pull out. Formal offer comes by letter, through the solicitor, and will include any items such as fixtures and fittings. The letter forms part of contract of sale.

Exchange of missives

If the offer is accepted, a formal letter called qualified acceptance is returned by the sellers solicitor, confirming or amending the conditions. The entry date may need to be negotiated to suit both parties. These formal letters are referred to as missives and may go back and forth for clarification.

Missives concluded

Once all the conditions are agreed, the purchase is then legally binding for both buyer and seller. The missives are concluded by the acting solicitors: neither the buyer or the seller signs anything. There is no deposit paid in the Scottish system except if you are buying a new house from a property developer

The law states that once the missives have been concluded, the purchaser is responsible for the insurance of the property. However, it is more usual for an agreement to be made in the missives that the seller remains liable until the date of entry.

The date that you would like to move is suggested in your formal offer to the seller. In this time you should be able to sell your house and complete any legal work. Before the date of entry, your solicitor will prepare what is known as a disposition to confirm the change of ownership. He will obtain from the sellers solicitor the title deeds which will be signed by the seller to agree the change of ownership. These will be handed over on the date of entry following payment of the property price.

Searches

There are two types of searches in Scotland:
Immediately prior to exchanging missives a search on the property and against the individual is made. This checks that the seller has a good title to the property and that the purchaser can grant security for the loan. In addition, a local authority search forms part of the missives. It checks that there are no proposed developments that would affect the property.

Selling a house or flat
Ways of selling your home

The majority of houses are bought and sold through solicitor offices, but you also have the options of selling through an estate agent or selling it privately yourself. Whatever option you choose, it is customary in Scotland to show prospective buyers around the house and explain the details.

DIY selling

This involves setting the price, preparing the sales details about the house, advertising it and showing people around. The advantages of this kind of sale are that you cut out middlemen and save commission.

However, you will need a solicitor for conveyancing.

Selling through an estate agent

These are normally Scottish branches of well-known chains of agents. They offer a service similar to their English counterparts. In contrast to selling through a solicitor, estate agents often encourage you to take the first offer rather than generating interest and setting a closing date. You should get quotes from agents about their charges. this will be typically around 1.5% of selling price.

Selling through a solicitor

Most property in Scotland is sold through solicitors. They provide a service similar to estate agents and have property centres displaying details of houses for sale, although there may be an extra one off charge for this depending on the area you are in. Their commission charges are often slightly cheaper than those of estate agents. It is normal practice to use the same solicitor to sell your house and carry out the legal side of the sale.

The selling process

Your solicitor or estate agent will prepare the sales particulars and discuss the selling price with you as part of their contract. Depending upon the circumstances, they will advise as to whether the house is sold as "offers above" or as "fixed price". The former is usually set slightly below the expected price to encourage buyers. If a degree of competitiveness is created you may be able to set a "closing" date which usually achieves a better selling price.

Legally you should leave all fixtures and fittings, such as carpets and curtains or kitchen equipment unless you draw up a contract which states otherwise.

The legal services of a solicitor

There are two main areas the solicitor will need to follow up to allow smooth progress of a house sale.

The title deeds will need to be examined to check that you are the true owner of the property. Scottish law includes the Matrimonial Homes (Family Protection) (Scotland) Act: even if only one spouse owns the property permission to sell must be given by the partner.

Conveyancing will involve property surveys, and local searches to check there are no proposals for developments. If you are using a solicitor to sell your house, they may offer an overall charge that covers selling and legal services.

Accepting offers

Your solicitor will inform you if anyone has shown an interest in your property. If a lot of interest is shown in your house, you could consider setting a closing date for offers. Your solicitor or estate agent should advise you whether this is a good idea. There is no point in setting a date until you are sure more than one person is likely to make a formal offer. The closing date is a specific time on a specific day that all formal offers will be assessed. You are not obliged to accept any offer if they are too low. Nor does the highest offer have to be accepted.

If you accept the highest offer, your solicitor may negotiate points concerning other conditions, such as extras included or dates, but there must be no attempt to try to raise the price offered. If you are using an estate agent, their role ends once the offer has been handed over to the solicitor.

A formal offer will include all the conditions of sale, the price, any items included, and the date of entry. Some offers are made with a time limit in which you must accept verbally, which can be as little as within 24 hours. You should seek advice from your solicitors whether to act promptly. You may be advised to hold out for a higher offer. If the purchaser is seriously interested they will not mind waiting for an acceptance. Your solicitor will engage in the process of exchanging missives with the buyers solicitor. Missives are formal letters laying down conditions of sale and may be passed back and forth until an amicable agreement is reached. Once final missives have been exchanged the contract is legally binding for both parties, so it is important that you are familiar with all the conditions being negotiated by your solicitor through the missives. It will be too late once they have finally been changed.

Setting an entry date

The date for finalising the sale is suggested by both the seller and by the buyer in his offer. It is negotiated by both parties and a mutually agreed date is written into the missives. This is the date when the keys are handed to your solicitor, and you must move out. Although the date of entry is set by the seller, it may need to be changed to achieve a compromise which suits you and the purchaser.

Completion

Title deeds. Your buyer's solicitor will need to prepare the disposition and for this your solicitor will send the title deeds. The disposition is the document that states the change of ownership on the title deeds, and will need to be signed by you. It is handed over to the purchaser's solicitor in exchange for payment of the property on the date of settlement.

Now read the Key Points from Chapter Eight overleaf.

****

Key Points From Chapter 8

1   The process of buying and selling property in Scotland is quite different to that in England.

2   Property in Scotland does not exist as freehold or leasehold. Instead a Feudal tenure exists.

3   "Gazumping" is not possible in Scotland. Once an offer is made it is virtually binding.

4   Solicitors play a very important part in the process of buying and selling property in Scotland.

9

Buying Overseas

Thousands of Britons have purchased properties overseas. However, this can be problematic and certainly basic advice is needed relating to the particular country where you are buying. There are a few general tips when buying abroad:

- Buy through a qualified and licensed agent. In most countries including France, Spain, Portugal and the USA, agents legally have to be licensed and using an unlicensed agent means that there is no comeback if things go wrong.
- Do not sign anything until you are sure that you understand it. Note that estate agents in the above countries will tend to do more of the legal work than in Britain and hence charge more commission.
- Always hire a solicitor (English speaking if you are not fluent in the local language) to act for you. In some countries, the locals do not use solicitors but you should insist. The solicitor will check that the seller owns the property and that there are no debts attached to it and that planning regulations have been met. Local searches are not as regulated as they are in the UK and it's often a case of making informal enquiries at the local town hall.
- Understand the role played by the state notary (notaire in France, notario in Spain) he or she is a state official, whose only role is to see that the sale is completed. He or she will not act for you or the seller.

There are a number of useful websites where more information can be gained:

www.french-property-news.com
This site is the online arm of the magazine French Property News. It claims to have the most comprehensive list of properties on the web and also has details of other organisations.

www.french-property.com

Similar to the above

www.europropertynet.com

This is a European wide estate agency service, carrying a wide range of properties from around Europe, including France, Spain, Portugal and Greece. Other advice is also available on this site.

For property in Spain, try www.spanishpropertyco.co.uk which specialises in retirement property.

For property in Eastern Europe you should go to www.eurobrix.com

Other useful websites:
For the USA-

www.primelocation.com
www.propertyshowrooms.com
www.escape2usa.co.uk

Property overseas generally
www.property-abroad.com

There are many other websites dealing with buying and selling property in most countries of the world. It goes without saying that you should learn as much about a country as possible and deal with professionals only before taking the plunge overseas.

Useful addresses and websites

The Buying Process

The Local Government Association
www.lganet.gov.uk
Confederation of Scottish Local Authorities
www.cosla.gov.uk
Greater London Authority
www.london.gov.uk
The Environment Agency
www.environment-agency.gov.uk
www.homecheckuk.com

House Prices

Halifax www.halifax.co.uk
Nationwide www.nationwide.co.uk
Land Registry www.landreg.gov.uk

Buying agents

Home Search Bureau www.homesearchbureau.co.uk

Property search sites

www.hometrack.co.uk
www.rightmove.co.uk
www.assertahome.co.uk
www.propertyfinder.co.uk

www.primelocation.com
www.findaproperty.com
www.thisislondon.co.uk

The buying and selling process

The Law Society www.lawsoc.org.uk
The Council of Mortgage Lenders www.cml.org.uk
HM Customs and Revenue www.inlandrevenue.co.uk

Scotland

Law Society of Scotland www.scotlaw.org.uk

Leasehold/freehold

Lease www.lease-advice.org
Association of Residential Managing Agents
www.arma.org.uk

Mortgage search sites/brokers

Money facts www.moneyfacts.co.uk
www.moneysupermarket.co.uk
www.moneynet.co.uk

New homes

NHBC www.nhbc.co.uk
National Home Owners Association www. nhoa.com

Renting and Letting

Association of Residential Letting Agencies (ARLA)
ARLA Administration
Maple House
53-55 Woodside Road
Amersham
Bucks
HP6 6AA
Tel: 01923 896555
Website: www.arla.co.uk
Email: info@arla.co.uk

Specialist rental property sites
www.letonthenet.com
www.lettingweb.com

Auctions
www.propwatch.com

****

Index

Amenity Land, 47
Architects and Surveyors Institute, 28
Area, 3, 11, 92
Areas of Outstanding Natural Beauty, 18
Association of Building Engineers, 28
Auctions, 43, 120

Bankruptcy, 6, 100, 101
Brokers, 5, 58
Budgeting, 33
Building Guarantees, 19
Building insurance, 52
Building Land, 46
Building societies, 57
Buildings insurance, 38
Buying a listed building, 3, 17
Buying abroad, 115
Buying an old house, 3, 15
Buying Overseas, 7, 115
Buying with a friend, 4, 42
Buy-to-let investors, 46

Cashbacks, 66
Centralised lenders, 5, 57
Chartered Institute of Arbitrators 020 7421 7455, 67
Choosing your property, 3, 12
Coal mining search, 92

Commercial Investments, 47
Commonhold, 13, 14, 84
Commonhold and Leasehold Reform Act 2002, 13, 14
Completing a sale, 4, 43
Completion, 6, 7, 98, 112
Conservation areas, 17
Consumer Protection from Unfair Trading Regulations 2008, 28
Contract for sale, 94
Conveyancing, 5, 35, 81, 102, 111
Costs of moving, 39

Death of Vendor, 101
Deposit, 4, 33
Deposits, 5, 60
Developers, 45
Disabled facilities grant, 3, 16

Endowment, 63, 64
Energy Performance Certificates, 4, 36
Energy Performance Certificates (EPC's), 36
English Heritage, 17
Equalities Act 2010, 3, 16
Estate Agents, 3, 5, 13, 27, 28, 33
Exchange of contracts, 4, 42
Exchange of missives, 7, 108
Exchanging contracts, 6, 98

Finance, 50
Financial advisors, 58
Financial Conduct Authority (FCA, 59

Financial Ombudsman Service, 67
Financial Services Act 1986, 94
Flipping, 45
Forced sales, 45
Foreign currency mortgages, 66
Freehold property, 5, 81
French Property News, 116

Garage blocks, 47

Georgian Group, 15
Ground rents, 45

Halifax, 13, 30, 118
Help to Buy Scheme, 5, 22, 60
Historic Scotland, 17
House swapping, 4, 53
Houses in multiple occupation, 46

Incorporated Society of Valuers and Auctioneers, 28
Industrial units, 47
Insurance, 4
Interest only mortgage, 65
investment properties, 45

Joint mortgages, 63
Joint sole agents, 29

Land Certificate, 87
Land Registration Acts of 1925, 86

Land Registry, 13, 36, 40, 86, 87, 118
Law of Property Act (Miscellaneous provisions) 1988, 94
Leasehold, 119
Leasehold property, 5, 82
Leasehold Reform Act 1993, 3, 14
Legal ownership of property, 5, 81
Legal pack, 50
Lenders, 5, 50, 57, 58, 60, 67, 119
Local authority properties, 45
Local authority searches, 6, 91
Local Land Charges Act 1975, 90
Local land charges search, 6, 88, 90

Making an offer, 4, 7, 41, 108
Misdescription, 6, 96
Misrepresentation, 6, 96, 97
Missives concluded, 7, 108
Mixed mortgages, 65
Mixed Use Properties, 47
Mortgage, 50
Mortgage arrangement fees, 38
Mortgage fees, 4, 38
Mortgage indemnity insurance, 38
Mortgage Market Review, 59
Multiple agency, 29

National Energy Services Scheme, 18
Non-disclosure, 6, 97

Pension mortgages, 65

Planning permission, 3, 16
Probates, 45
Property investors, 44
Property Misdescriptions Act 2010, 27
Purchasing a flat, 3, 13
Receivership sales, 45

Registered land, 86
Removals, 4, 39
Removers, 104
Renovation grants, 3, 16
Repayment mortgages, 65
Repossessions, 44, 45
Residential Investments, 46
Retail shops, 47
Right to Buy, 19, 20
Royal Institute of British Architects, 15
Royal Institute of Chartered Surveyors, 13, 15
Rural areas, 11

Sale by tender, 4, 52, 53
Scotland, 7, 17, 106, 107, 109, 110, 111, 114, 119
Secretary of State for Scotland, 17
Secretary of State for Wales, 17
Self-build, 3, 23
Service charges, 13
Services, 18, 66, 67, 68, 94
Shared ownership property, 22
Social Homebuy, 21
Social Housing, 22

Sole agency selling., 29
Spain, 115, 116
Special Conditions of Sale, 50
Stamp duty, 4, 34, 35, 40
Structural surveys, 4, 37

Tenanted Properties, 46
The 1996 Housing Act, 13
The National House Building Council, 18
Transport links, 11

Unique Properties, 47
Urban areas, 11
USA, 115, 116

Valuing a property, 3, 12
Victorian Society, 15
Viewing properties, 3, 14

Yuppification, 11